THE Kittie Knox PLAYS

Patrick Gabridge,
Claire Soleil Gardner, and
Kirsten Greenidge

Patrick Gabridge, Claire Soleil Gardner, and Kirsten Greenidge

Published by Plays in Place
44 Willow Street, #2
Florence, MA 01062
617-959-1437
www.playsinplace.com

Cover Image and Design by Jules Talbot
Text Design and Layout by Abella Publishing Services, LLC
Editing by Talya Kingston

All photos are by Ben Rose Photography, with the exception of:
Sami Ahmad, page iv

First edition: April 2026

ISBN: 978-0-9986982-5-0

CONTENTS

INTRODUCTIONS

This project exists because of the tenacity of author/historian/enthusiast Larry J. Finison, who, back in May of 2022, introduced me to Kittie Knox's story, as he searched for someone who might want to turn it into a play. The more I heard and read, the clearer it became that her spirit and persistence were exactly what Plays in Place needed to explore.

Thus began a long and convoluted process for what became one of our most complex projects. Our writers developed their scripts with the help of dozens of actors, guided by our tireless director, Michelle Aguillon, through readings and workshops, always working towards our first "bike-specific play." Larry has remained an ever-present source of historical information and enthusiasm. The use of actual bikes felt critical to capture the vigor of the 1890s cycling boom and of Kittie and her friends. We decided to stage the plays more like a cycling event, in a single day at a single location, hopefully in spots with some relation to Kittie and/or cycling. To increase the level of difficulty, we chose to perform in three different towns over the course of three weeks. Our lead producer, Hannah McEachern, jumped on board this project late in the game and managed to juggle all the moving parts in what was an incredible experience for all of us.

MassBike was an integral part of the process from the beginning, as we navigated different sites and mounted a significant fundraising effort. More than 90 individual donors and half a dozen foundation and corporate sponsors contributed the funds necessary to produce the plays for their 2025 premiere. The three sites, managed by DivcoWest, Historic New England, and the Friends of Herter Park, were fully supportive of this unique project. I will be eternally grateful to our donors and our sites for their generosity.

That initial production was not the final word on these plays. From the very beginning, it was our intention to publish a book that includes the scripts, program notes and photos, and historical infomation, so that we could share the stories of Kittie and her friends as widely as possible. Now, you're holding these stories in

Hampton Richards

your hands. Our hope is that members of bike clubs, theatres, and schools will be inspired to produce these plays for their communities.

These plays are set at a time in America when Black people's rights were being increasingly restricted, through violence as well as through laws and adverse Supreme Court decisions. Women were struggling not just for the right to vote, but also for their bodily and personal autonomy. All while new technologies were rapidly changing everyday life in ways that often felt disorienting. These plays and Kittie's vibrant, indomitable spirit in the face of governmental and cultural barriers feel increasingly relevant with every passing day. I hope we can all be inspired by her courage and the joy she found in the world.

—Patrick Gabridge,
Producing Artistic Director,
Plays in Place & playwright
(*Welcome to Asbury Park*)

Patrick Gabridge

Born in 1874, Kittie Knox's life parallels the dramatic rise and decline of bicycling in the nineteenth century—the cycling "Craze."

Modern cycling developed on the Continent and in England in the early 1870s. High wheel bicycles (typically big wheels in front and little wheels in back) were soon imported to America. They were stable but if a rider "took a header," it was an injurious trip to the ground. In 1878, high wheeling gentlemen started the Boston Bicycle Club—first in the nation. During the 1880s women rode large-wheeled tricycles but in their long dresses they moved slowly.

By the early 1890s, most cyclists had switched over to "safety" bicycles with equal sized tires, chains, and pneumatic tubes. Much safer and faster. But women were still at a disadvantage because of the heavier curved frame required to accommodate long skirts. Some women (including Kittie) began to ride men's bikes and wear bloomers or knickerbockers.

Kittie, a dexterous seamstress, dancer, and cyclist, knew all about the cycling world. Her West End Boston apartment was within blocks of the League of American Wheelmen headquarters on Atlantic Avenue (Kittie joined the L.A.W. around 1893); the offices of Mary Sargent Hopkins' *The Wheelwoman* magazine overlooked Boston Common on Tremont Street; and Bicycle Row—a string of bicycle stores on Columbus Avenue. Chief among these was Albert Pope's Columbia brand bicycle. Just off Tremont Street in the South End was the clubhouse of the all-women's Bostonian Cycle Club. Close by Kittie in the North End were the Boston Italian Wheelmen. In the heart of the largely Black and immigrant West End, and down the street from her home (at the corner of Irving and Cambridge streets—now a Starbucks), was the Bowdoin Street armory of Company L of the Sixth Massachusetts Volunteer Militia, with its own Bicycle Corps, including members of the Riverside Cycle Club—Kittie's companions on many rides. The Charles Street AME Church was just around the corner. The church hosted protests against increasing anti-Black violence in the South—and against the L.A.W. Constitutional Amendment of 1894, banning new Black members. Attempts by Boston cyclists, both Black and White, failed to dislodge the rule. This set off Kittie's confrontation at Asbury Park, New Jersey. Kittie rode fast and long century

(100-mile) rides, but the L.A.W. forbade women from racing, fearing "bicycle face" and "bicycle hump" and masculinizing women, so no races were ever recorded for her.

Kittie continued to sew, dance, and cycle through the late 1890s. But bicycling rapidly declined and the L.A.W. largely disbanded. New modes of transportation and recreation came along like streetcars, country clubs, motorcycles, and automobiles, and that ended the "Craze."

—Lorenz J. Finison,
Historical Consultant

Lorenz J. Finison

THE PLAYS

To the Cliffs of Gay Head

by Kirsten Greenidge

Characters

Katherine (Kittie) Knox

Benzina Reese (later Benzina Gray)

Viola Wheaton (soon to be Viola Hamilton)

Mary Sargent Hopkins

"Miss Merrie Wheeler" (an invention of the writing of Mary Sargent Hopkins)

Charles (Charley) Percival

William Hamilton

Robert Teamoh

TO THE CLIFFS OF GAY HEAD

Part 1

Ocean Park in Cottage City (Oak Bluffs), Martha's Vineyard, 1893.

In real life, there is a bandstand and well-kept grass and newly paved paths.

It's mid-summer.

The ocean is in sight.

If possible, the sound of surf, soft.

If possible, the sound of gulls, also soft.

(We see Viola first. She cycles into the sight line of the audience, stops her bicycle with her feet.)

VIOLA: *(to audience)* I spent the summer of 1893, by the sea.

If possible, the sound of surf, soft.

If possible, the sound of gulls, also soft. (Perhaps a speaker in her bicycle's basket.)

VIOLA: *(to audience, her words buoyed by warm air and vacation excitement)* Cottage City, Martha's Vineyard. Benzina—

(Benzina begins to cycle into sight, from behind the audience.)

And me—

BENZINA: *(Calling)* Viola. Viola. Wait up now.

(Benzina cycles to Viola.)

VIOLA: *(to audience)* And Kittie.

(Kittie zooms in, circles and tricks and pure energy. Kittie wears a cycling costume with bloomers, but Benzina and Viola wear cycling outfits with skirts.)

(While Viola and Benzina's bicycles may have a few feminine flairs, Kittie's bike is a man's bike. To ride it well, she leans her body over its handlebars, not feminine but very effective.)

KITTIE: Don't even think of stopping now. We're going clear to the Cliffs of Gay Head.

BENZINA: You go clear to the Cliffs. That's the whole length of Martha's Vineyard.

(Benzina plants her feet on the ground, breathes in deeply.)

KITTIE: Oh, it's not even that far.

BENZINA: On dirt roads? It so does too feel that far. Somehow this is the same ocean as Boston, but it smells one thousand times more sweet.

VIOLA: *(to audience)* Just girls. Barely out of plaits and hair ribbons.

KITTIE: Benzina Reese, this island may as well be one thousand miles from Boston. Fresh air.

Open roads—

(Kittie is mid-trick/fast circle. . .)

VIOLA: *(to Kittie)* Careful. Careful now.

KITTIE: Viola, who do you know that's gotten anywhere by being careful?

VIOLA: You just go so fast.

KITTIE: Tell me another way to go, and I'll tell you the truth: I'd rather go blind.

BENZINA: Kittie.

KITTIE: Why do we have legs if we shouldn't use them?

VIOLA: Is that why you keep showing yours off, for any and everyone to see?

BENZINA: Viola.

VIOLA: "Bloomers."

(Kittie dismounts her bicycle with a flourish.)

KITTIE: Knickerbockers.

VIOLA: Like a man.

BENZINA: Oh heavens, Kittie is not a man.

KITTIE: You like them. How can you not like them? You love them. I'll whip you up a pair.

BENZINA: *(Looking at Kittie's outfit)* They are a little daring.

KITTIE: They are a lot daring.

VIOLA: What respectable lady wears pants like a man?

BENZINA: The same type of lady who rides a man's bicycle and isn't ashamed to look like a brute doing so.

KITTIE: More power with a man's bicycle. I could speed my way to West Chop, Tisbury, and yes ma'am all the way to Gay Head on this bike, with you two trailing behind.

VIOLA: You won't catch me in anybody's bloomers, even if you do sew yours beautifully, Kittie.

BENZINA: Yes, you sure can sew.

KITTIE: Bloomers, knickerbockers, short skirts, are the wave of the future.

VIOLA: Who lets people see their knees? No one respectable we know.

KITTIE: You mark my words: this is the full blown, electric-light future. The living, the most alive future. Not everyone is almost dead because they got engaged.

BENZINA: Ooh, your tongue is wicked today.

VIOLA: Sure is.

(Viola looks at Kittie. Kittie looks at Viola. Benzina laughs. Kittie and Viola follow, laugh too.)

BENZINA: We're happy for you, Viola. You will be a beautiful bride.

VIOLA: Thank you, Benzina.

BENZINA: And William is a lucky man.

KITTIE: He's more than lucky.

VIOLA: William is a catch, Kittie. Don't you start in on him being otherwise.

KITTIE: William better realize what he's getting.

VIOLA: Who says I'm something to be "gotten"?

BENZINA: Kittie, don't start anything, now.

KITTIE: Who's starting?

BENZINA: Viola looks dainty and sweet, but I think she could take you, if you hit a last nerve.

VIOLA: *(A little bit of a front)* Ooh, she hasn't hit any of my nerves.

KITTIE: *(to Benzina)* See?

VIOLA: Yet.

BENZINA: Ha.

KITTIE: Will Hamilton better know how much of a catch you are. That is what I mean.

VIOLA: He knows.

KITTIE: Your singing—

VIOLA: *(Proud)* I do carry a tune.

KITTIE: All your music, to be truthful.

BENZINA: You sure can play a piano, Viola.

VIOLA: Why thank you.

KITTIE: And your writing—

VIOLA: William knows who he's marrying. Trust me.

BENZINA: It isn't right to drag the poor man. He lost a wife—

KITTIE: That doesn't mean he needs to go and collect a new one, just like that.

VIOLA: I am not being gotten or collected or—I'm going to be alright, Kittie, you'll see.

(Viola looks at Kittie. This may be too much earnestness for Kittie.)

KITTIE: I'm just saying if I had all those lessons, and schooling— You've even traveled on tours, played all over the country.

VIOLA: If by "the country" you mean Ohio, then yes, you are correct.

KITTIE: Don't discredit yourself. It's like disrespecting yourself—

VIOLA: I'm not. *(But maybe she is?)*

KITTIE: Shout about all you've accomplished all over the place, 'til you're hoarse in the throat and blue in the face.

VIOLA: You're so spirited, Kittie. What would we do without you?

BENZINA: Rest.

(Benzina and Viola laugh.)

(As Kittie continues, Benzina takes a blanket out of her bicycle basket, preparing for a rest stop.)

KITTIE: No, no, I mean it, now. Viola, you are, you're accomplished.

VIOLA: And so is William.

BENZINA: William Hamilton is vice president of our esteemed club.

VIOLA: Just look at all the Riverside Cycling Club has done all spring, since its creation in April. Boston's only Colored cycling club. It's a special thing, Kittie—

KITTIE: I'm not saying it's not.

VIOLA: Look how many clubs won't allow us.

KITTIE: You don't have to tell me.

VIOLA: No Colored, no women.

(Benzina holds up the blanket.)

BENZINA: I took this out to give you all a hint.

VIOLA: William even says in the fall, Riverside is going to host a century ride. One hundred miles into the country. Farther than Framingham, than Westboro; out clear past Worcester even.

BENZINA: I say we sit a spell.

VIOLA: "Sit a spell." Now that's South Carolina if I ever heard it.

BENZINA: Well ma'am, you can take a girl out of Carolina, but you can't take one bit of Carolina out of the girl.

KITTIE: *(Not done with their last subject)* I mean it.

VIOLA: Mean what? What do you mean?

KITTIE: He's old.

BENZINA: Oh, he is not either.

VIOLA: He's just a few years older than I am.

KITTIE: No, no, we are young. We are all young. You get married and it's cooking and tidying up after someone else—

(Benzina holds up a lunch pail/bucket from her bicycle's basket.)

BENZINA: I've got fried chicken from Mrs. Hemmings'.

(But Kittie hasn't moved. And neither has Viola.)

BENZINA: And apples from—

VIOLA: You have a lot to say about a lot that isn't your business.

BENZINA: I'm serious you all, I am not riding out to West Chop, Tisbury, Gay Head, nowhere, if we don't eat and drink something first. I'll stay right here in the Inkwell until I get lunch in me.

VIOLA: Oh, do not call it that.

KITTIE: I like it.

VIOLA: It's very ugly.

BENZINA: Nothing wrong with it.

VIOLA: It's hateful. Calling the ocean where all of us swim a bottle of black ink.

KITTIE: See, see. This is what I'm talking about.

VIOLA: Oh, what now?

KITTIE: We are young. We are the future. We won't make any progress if we think of ourselves as the downtrodden all the time. What I think is—. What I think is—. When someone hits you with a punch? You counter punch. They call it the Inkwell to make fun of us, we take that name and become prideful of it. Sure, Riverside is a good thing, a special thing. But I'll be damned—

(Both Viola and Benzina gasp.)

KITTIE: I will be. If I'm not going to join the other clubs, too.

VIOLA: You can try.

BENZINA: They may let you in but they won't let you stay.

KITTIE: Who is a member of the L.A.W.? Me. I am a legal member of the League of American Wheelmen.

VIOLA: They'll show you the door. You'll see.

KITTIE: Their Massachusetts Division is meeting here in just a few days—

BENZINA: And you can bet they will be eyeballing that meeting door once they see you waltzing up to it.

VIOLA: *(Pretending to knock on a door)* Knock-knock—

BENZINA: *(Taking up the improv. . .)* Nobody here, not meeting here—

(Viola and Benzina laugh loudly.)

VIOLA: The National L.A.W. is already talking about a color bar against us folks. They Do Not Want Us. Not in their schools, not in their hotels, and especially not riding beside them on bicycles all day long and then sidling up to them once those rides are over—

KITTIE: Listen, listen to me now. The future is not bending to silly, old ways, customs. I'm a Coming Woman, a new woman—

VIOLA: The future is babies, and that is exactly what William and I intend to get working on right away.

(Viola and Benzina giggle, laugh.)

KITTIE: I will decline at present, thank you.

VIOLA: Don't I know it.

BENZINA: How many proposals do you reckon you've had?

KITTIE: There's that Carolina: "reckon."

VIOLA: This month or this year?

BENZINA: You cut a lovely figure, Kittie, all the fellows say so.

VIOLA: It's those bloomers. *(A joke)* Obscene.

KITTIE: I make every one of my skirts, blouses. If you know how to cut and stitch just so, you know how to accentuate oneself in all the very right ways.

VIOLA: You should let one of those fellows at least take you out one time—

(A quick look between Viola and Kittie.)

KITTIE: Sakes alive, that is one smooth ride out here on these paths. All that men-voting and the L.A.W. Good Roads campaign to smooth over these paths and streets sure is paying off.

BENZINA: Men-voting. Ha.

VIOLA: Women will not get the vote, Kittie. And don't speak so loud, the boy's bike is bad enough, you don't want to be tied up with the suffrage ladies, too.

(Viola shivers.)

KITTIE: Maybe I do.

(Kittie and Viola look at each other.)

BENZINA: All these cycling paths. Cottage City is the place to be.

(Kittie mounts her bike. Benzina sees her.)

BENZINA: No, Kittie, lunch.

KITTIE: I'm serious about the cliffs.

VIOLA: It's just dirt roads and treachery.

KITTIE: We could make it out before late afternoon, I know it.

(Kittie has begun cycling in circles. Benzina hurriedly puts her lunch items back in her bicycle basket.)

BENZINA: Oh, here we go. Viola, look at her go. Riding around in circles—

VIOLA: Like one of those poodles under a circus tent.

KITTIE: If all I had to do was cycle around a ring for my supper, I'd do it gladly, lickety-split.

(Kittie hunches over her handlebars, picks up some speed. Benzina hurries it up.)

KITTIE: West Chop, then the cliffs, come on.

(Viola looks at Kittie.)

VIOLA: It's just us girls. It's not a race.

KITTIE: Isn't it though?

(Kittie speeds off. Benzina rights herself on her cycle and follows.)

(Viola turns to the audience.)

VIOLA: *(to audience)* That was what was peculiar about Kittie. It was indeed always a race with her. The hard part was, figuring out who she thought she was racing against. Because the thing about Kittie was, if it was you she was racing against, you sure did feel it in your bones.

(Elsewhere, Mary Sargent Hopkins lets out a loud shriek and visible shiver.)

(Viola adjusts her collar, uncomfortable, but does not see or take in Mary Sargent Hopkins.)

BENZINA: *(Riding away)* VIOLA. WE GONNA LEAVE YOU.

(Viola cycles off.)

Part 2

Boston Common, Boston, Massachusetts, also Summer 1893.

(Mary Sargent Hopkins begins to walk a tight circle, pencil and paper in hand. As she speaks, "Miss Merrie Wheeler" rides alongside. "Miss Merrie Wheeler" wears a long skirt or cycling costume with skirt and leggings, but NOT bloomers. "Miss Merrie Wheeler" rides a lady's bicycle, all smiles, as if on a magazine cover, which, come 1895, she will be.)

MARY SARGENT HOPKINS: If there is any one thing I hate, it is a masculine woman.

("Miss Merrie Wheeler" stops, gives Mary Sargent Hopkins a "what?" look.)

MARY SARGENT HOPKINS: Not you, dear.

("Miss Merrie Wheeler" pats her sternum, assured, then continues to ride. Mary Sargent Hopkins taps pencil to paper.)

MARY SARGENT HOPKINS: I must be honest, my very heart breaks to see women donning knickerbockers—

("Miss Merrie Wheeler" stops riding, looks down at her outfit.)

MARY SARGENT HOPKINS: Not you, dear.

("Miss Merrie Wheeler" continues to ride.)

MARY SARGENT HOPKINS: *(As she writes)* What cycling has the ability to do for women is to provide exhilarating, and much needed, outdoor exercise.

("Miss Merrie Wheeler" stops, looks over the Mary Sargent Hopkins.)

MARY SARGENT HOPKINS: I said exercise, dear, don't stop, keep riding.

("Miss Merrie Wheeler" does.)

MARY SARGENT HOPKINS: *(Writing)* And I cannot overstate the importance, for women cyclists, to promote the proper decorum. In dress. In behavior.

("Miss Merrie Wheeler" raises her hand. But Mary Sargent Hopkins does not seem to see her.)

MARY SARGENT HOPKINS: For parents and girls, health should be the first consideration. There can never be a feeble mind in an active body. A woman who lives a full life is a woman who is a personal acquaintance of forest, field, and stream; of sunlight and fresh air. The wheel can bring women closer to physical perfection.

("Miss Merrie Wheeler" clears her throat, still riding. As she does, she begins to circle, perhaps rides with a bit more gusto.)

MARY SARGENT HOPKINS: Down with the hunched form brought on from sewing, and horseback riding—

("Miss Merrie Wheeler" clears her throat again, rings her bicycle's bell. Mary Sargent Hopkins turns to "Miss Merrie Wheeler.")

MARY SARGENT HOPKINS: What. What is it, my dear?

(She notices "Miss Merrie Wheeler" is circling and has a hunched body.)

MARY SARGENT HOPKINS: AHHHHHH.

"MISS MERRIE WHEELER": AHHHHHH.

("Miss Merrie Wheeler" takes a tumble.)

"MISS MERRIE WHEELER": *(From the ground)* Oh my.

MARY SARGENT HOPKINS: And that is exactly what occurs when one goes racing about. A wheel is not meant to turn a woman into an indecent spectacle.

"MISS MERRIE WHEELER": Oh. I do apologize. I didn't realize.

MARY SARGENT HOPKINS: "You didn't realize."

"MISS MERRIE WHEELER": It was fun.

MARY SARGENT HOPKINS: It was indecent.

"MISS MERRIE WHEELER": I am very sorry.

MARY SARGENT HOPKINS: You are me, and I am you.

"MISS MERRIE WHEELER": Yes, I understand.

MARY SARGENT HOPKINS: And I assure you I would never scorch about, letting any manliness jump around in broad daylight like that.

"MISS MERRIE WHEELER": Should I come back out in the dark? I could light a little lamp. Put it right on my handlebars.

MARY SARGENT HOPKINS: How could this happen?

Jennifer Drummond and Em Sheeran

"MISS MERRIE WHEELER": Of course, if I were to fall then, my skirts and hair might burn to a crisp. But I've seen the men ride like that. So, I believe I could do it if I were to give it a try. *(This was the wrong thing to say.)*

MARY SARGENT HOPKINS: Give it a try?

"MISS MERRIE WHEELER": Um, yes?

MARY SARGENT HOPKINS: Give it a try?

"MISS MERRIE WHEELER": Um, no?

MARY SARGENT HOPKINS: This cannot happen. You are me, and I am you.

"MISS MERRIE WHEELER": I'm afraid I actually don't understand.

MARY SARGENT HOPKINS: *(À la Sophia from The Golden Girls)* Picture it.

"MISS MERRIE WHEELER": *(Skeptical)* Alright.

MARY SARGENT HOPKINS: In the future a few years from now.

"MISS MERRIE WHEELER": Alright.

MARY SARGENT HOPKINS: I use the good name I have built expounding on the advantages of bicycling.

"MISS MERRIE WHEELER": Mrs. Mary Sargent Wheeler. *(She puts a hand to her cheek)* Oh my goodness. I knew that. How did I know that?

MARY SARGENT HOPKINS: I will use that name—from my lectures and articles—and I will conduct the most influential women's cycling bulletin known to all.

"MISS MERRIE WHEELER": Well, that's impossible, there are tens, hundreds.

MARY SARGENT HOPKINS: Not like mine, there aren't.

"MISS MERRIE WHEELER": Yours? What about me?

MARY SARGENT HOPKINS: Well, I will not use my own name.

"MISS MERRIE WHEELER": This hardly sounds worthy if you won't use your own name.

MARY SARGENT HOPKINS: You will be my pen name.

"MISS MERRIE WHEELER": Merrie Wheeler.

MARY SARGENT HOPKINS: Merrie Wheeler. The quintessential Wheel Woman. Devoted to health and home. Yes. See? The bicycle is the great emancipator for women otherwise doomed to ill health and ill spirit. It will be my purpose to make every woman a convert. And, it makes men more moral, too.

"MISS MERRIE WHEELER": Merrie Wheeler. Hey, I like that.

MARY SARGENT HOPKINS: But you mustn't ride like a fool.

"MISS MERRIE WHEELER": What?

MARY SARGENT HOPKINS: There are those who seem to use the wheel in, in the most grotesque of ways.

"MISS MERRIE WHEELER": Oh, that sounds just terrible.

MARY SARGENT HOPKINS: Back hunched, body confined in bloomers—

"MISS MERRIE WHEELER": Knickerbockers.

MARY SARGENT HOPKINS: Like a schoolboy.

"MISS MERRIE WHEELER": Going fast was fun.

MARY SARGENT HOPKINS: Grotesque.

"MISS MERRIE WHEELER": When you put it that way.

MARY SARGENT HOPKINS: Yes, I've read all about the likes of Miss Kittie Knox. Speeding around, riding with men as if she is one of them. I'm not against the Colored women enjoying the magnificent sport of cycling. I'm not against any of the Colored people at all. When I was a girl, in Lynn, I remember some of the great abolitionists lived almost right next door. That stays with a person, growing up near such greatness. But Miss Kittie Knox is not a credit to her race, far, far from it. She is no more a prime exemplar of her race, of her sex, then a flea.

"MISS MERRIE WHEELER": Do we write that? That … does not seem very nice.

MARY SARGENT HOPKINS: Mark my words. She is cunning. She is a disgrace. The sooner a woman knows her role, the happier she will be. You will see.

(Mary Sargent Hopkins spans her palms up and out into the air, à la Sophia again. "Miss Merrie Wheeler" follows with her gaze. "Miss Merrie Wheeler" breaks the moment.)

"MISS MERRIE WHEELER": Can I, um, keep riding?

MARY SARGENT HOPKINS: Of course, my dear. Of course.

(Mary Sargent Hopkins continues to write as she walks. "Miss Merrie Wheeler" cycles, but gets a little too forceful, maybe does a circle or hunches her shoulders. Mary Sargent Hopkins admonishes "Miss Merrie Wheeler" with a look. "Miss Merrie Wheeler" straightens up, rides upright with impeccable posture.)

MARY SARGENT HOPKINS: There's a nice girl. Perfect.

(Mary Sargent Hopkins and "Miss Merrie Wheeler" walk/ride off.)

Part 3

*West Medford, Massachusetts, in front of the home of
William Overton, later in the summer.*

*(We hear William Hamilton and Robert Teamoh's voices
before we see them, walking their bicycles.)*

WILLIAM: No, no, no, no. no.

ROBERT: You are missing your sweetheart, that is why you are
this disagreeable.

WILLIAM: Don't you worry about my sweetheart.

ROBERT: It's a fast scene, out there on Martha's Vineyard.

WILLIAM: And now you are disrespecting my sweetheart?

ROBERT: Viola is a lovely girl. I am disrespecting no one.

WILLIAM: You will never get a law like that passed. That is why I
am so disagreeable. If we want real change, we must not be
foolhardy about it.

ROBERT: Did you vote for me or not?

WILLIAM: A man's vote is his own matter.

ROBERT: You must trust me. No one should be refused service or
accommodations because of his skin. This is lunacy. There are
only so many houses like Overton's.

*(Robert nods his head in the direction of where Overton's home
could be.)*

WILLIAM: I am grateful for Overton. One gets this far out of
Boston, Cambridge, one never knows who is a friend—

ROBERT: And who might have you beat.

WILLIAM: Well, I wouldn't like to put it so harshly.

ROBERT: It is harsh. It is very harsh. *(A new tack)* Don't you want to
know Viola, when she heads out on one of those lady's rides—

WILLIAM: I don't think the Riverside Club should be doing much
of those.

Audience

ROBERT: Don't you think Viola, or any children you have after you're married this fall, deserve to be safe wherever they choose to lay their heads?

WILLIAM: I don't know if I want a wife of mine riding all over the countryside.

ROBERT: Says the man whose sweetheart is one of the graceful summer girls being written up in the papers.

WILLIAM: Wherever that Kittie goes, she draw attention. Yes, I heard word of it same as you. "Graceful cycling" from Miss Kittie Knox and Miss Viola Wheaton. I'm not sure I want my wife zipping about, being written up in newspapers.

ROBERT: Viola and Kittie and Benzina, all the girls, deserve to go wherever they please, without harassment.

WILLIAM: That paper claimed they're Riverside members.

ROBERT: I know we see eye to eye on this, my friend.

WILLIAM: But since when does Riverside have women members?

ROBERT: You can't believe all you read, Mr. Hamilton.

WILLIAM: Aren't you a newspaperman, Mr. Teamoh?

ROBERT: Adding to our laws, increasing the penalty for doing such a thing, that is the way forward.

WILLIAM: You propose that in the legislature, and you will be voted out.

ROBERT: Not by Ward 9, our West End loves me.

(Just then, Charles (Charley) Percival comes racing by, feet off his pedals . . . WOOOOOSH.)

CHARLEY: Heeeeeeeeeyyyyyyyyyyyyyyy.

(William and Robert watch him. William calls out.)

WILLIAM: Charley Percival?

(Charles Percival races by again.)

CHARLEY: Heeeeeeeeeyyyyyyyyyyyyyyy.

ROBERT: What brings you out to West Medford, Mr. Percival?

(Charles Percival comes to a stop.)

CHARLEY: Oh, just getting the lay of the land.

WILLIAM: Out here?

CHARLEY: Why not out here?

ROBERT: Of course you're always welcome.

CHARLEY: Beautiful countryside.

WILLIAM: Sure is.

CHARLEY: For those who know it.

ROBERT: Although I can't say many of the, uh, lighter persuasion usually know it. Out here at Overton's, that is.

WILLIAM: Yes, not many of the Whiter persuasion usually venture to this side of Medford, to a Colored boarding house—

CHARLEY: Storm's brewing. Cycling is in my blood. Passed down to me from my father—

WILLIAM: The first bicycle shop in Boston.

ROBERT: Columbus Avenue.

CHARLEY: *(to William)* Beautiful thing, your Riverside Club.

WILLIAM: We sure think so.

ROBERT: I'm trying to remind Mr. Hamilton here that a club is good, but it's not enough. We need more laws. You heard about the business with the barbershop.

CHARLEY: Yes, yes I did.

ROBERT: If a man asks for a service, whether that service is lodging or a meal or a visit to a barber, he should not be barred from that service.

Nathan Johnson, Dustin Teuber, Joshua Lee Robinson

CHARLEY: I agree.

ROBERT: Good.

CHARLEY: Wholeheartedly. But. I smell trouble. I smell a storm. I know this sport like the back of my hand. The way your girl, Kittie, rides—

WILLIAM: I assure you she is not either of our girls.

ROBERT: William here speaks the truth.

CHARLEY: And the figure she cuts.

(William and Robert look at Charles.)

CHARLEY: Striking. She's striking. And fearless. Keeps pace with the men, beats those men, and most of them are so smitten when she hops off her wheel they're either hopping mad or smitten and googly eyed. She's shaking everyone up. Mrs. Hopkins is fit to be tied just by the mention of her. You get those laws ready, Representative Teamoh. With that one around, you're gonna need them.

(Charles hops on his cycle and speeds away.)

Audience

Part 4

The sound of ocean, gulls.

A cliff above the sea, Gay Head (Aquinnah), Martha's Vineyard.

(Kittie stands, taking in the air. Benzina enters, walking her cycle.)

KITTIE: You won't catch me dead in a white dress at St. Augustine's. Never, never, never. And William Hamilton is old, Benzina. Maybe not in years, but in his soul.

BENZINA: It might be a good life.

KITTIE: Tuh.

BENZINA: And not everyone is able to make ends meet on their own.

KITTIE: Well, everyone should try.

(Kittie looks around, notices Viola is really nowhere to be found.)

KITTIE: Where'd she go?

BENZINA: Not everything's a race to the finish. Sometimes, you just need to stop, take it all in, not be so quick to push so.

KITTIE: Everyone around us is pushing. You can't tell me the way things are is the way they are forever meant to be.

BENZINA: Maybe.

KITTIE: No, you can't.

BENZINA: Even if I did, you wouldn't believe it.

KITTIE: No, Carolina, I wouldn't.

(Viola, panting, catches up, walking her bicycle.)

VIOLA: *(pant)* Gay *(pant)* Head *(pant)* Land *(pant)* Sakes *(pant)* Alive!

(Benzina laughs. Kittie looks at Viola.)

VIOLA: *(pant)* I'm tryina keep up with you, Kittie *(pant)* Lord knows I am.

(Kittie softens.)

(Benzina brings out some of the food from her lunch, breaks it in three.)

BENZINA: Told you there's gotta be rest some time.

(Benzina hands them food.)

KITTIE: Maybe.

(The three eat, look out over the cliff to the expanse of sky. Sound of surf.)

KITTIE: You'll make a beautiful bride, Viola Wheaton.

VIOLA: That's mighty kind of you, Miss Kittie Knox.

(Viola turns to the audience.)

VIOLA: That October, I married William Hamilton at St. Augustine's Church. But Charley Percival wasn't wrong. And Robert Teamoh wasn't wrong. Something was coming. We just didn't know what.

— End of Play —

Welcome to Asbury Park

by Patrick Gabridge

Characters

Kittie Knox

Benzina Reese

Viola (Wheaton) Hamilton

William Hamilton

Robert Teamoh

Charley Percival

Gertude Parker

Colonel W. W. Watts

Abbot Bassett

Mary Sargent Hopkins

Settings

The banks of the Charles River in Cambridge, Massachusetts;
a ship; the League of American Wheelmen (L.A.W.) meet in
Asbury Park, New Jersey.

Scene 1

(July 1895. Kittie, Benzina, Viola, William Hamilton, and Robert Teamoh are on a ride with the Riverside Cycle Club. Perhaps they circle the audience or pass by multiple times. Kittie is speedy and likes to ride with the men. Benzina and Viola move a bit more leisurely.)

(A whistle or a bugle sounds. The riders stop together and dismount, with the exception of Kittie, who still rides in circles. The women take picnic supplies from the baskets on their bikes.)

BENZINA: Kittie! Come eat with us.

VIOLA HAMILTON: That girl is happiest on a bicycle, no doubt about it.

KITTIE: I'm coming, I'm coming. I just hate to stop.

WILLIAM HAMILTON: Don't we know it.

(Kittie joins them.)

ROBERT TEAMOH: You do like to make an entrance.

BENZINA: I would, too, if I had a prize-winning outfit like that.

KITTIE: I can make you one. I'll give you the friends and family discount.

ROBERT TEAMOH: All the attention from the Waltham competition must be good for business.

VIOLA HAMILTON: Oh, she's famous now. It was in all the papers. "Colored Woman Beats White Women in Costume Contest."

WILLIAM HAMILTON: Maybe Kittie should endorse you in your re-election bid.

ROBERT TEAMOH: I need all the help I can get.

KITTIE: Just make sure to recommend me to the wives of the other legislators for their ball gowns. I need every dollar to pay for this trip.

ROBERT TEAMOH: What trip?

KITTIE: I'm thinking about going to the League of American Wheelmen's national meet in Asbury Park.

ROBERT TEAMOH: Thinking or planning?

WILLIAM HAMILTON: It starts in a few days and it's a very complicated journey.

KITTIE: I'll take the train to the ship, then sail overnight to New York, pedal across town, catch another ferry, board another train, and then I'll be there.

WILLIAM HAMILTON: Sounds expensive.

KITTIE: I've been sewing like crazy to save up. There will be thousands of cyclists from all across the country.

ROBERT TEAMOH: *(to Benzina)* Are you going with her?

BENZINA: No. I have to work. And—

ROBERT TEAMOH: And?

VIOLA HAMILTON: Benzina understands that we're not welcome there. Not at the meet, not in Asbury Park.

KITTIE: I will be fine. There will be riders from other Massachusetts clubs, people I've seen at meets on Martha's Vineyard for years.

VIOLA HAMILTON: White riders.

KITTIE: They will vouch for me.

ROBERT TEAMOH: Will they?

BENZINA: *(to the men)* Why aren't one of you going to the National Meet? Your presence would make a statement?

KITTIE: Yes, come with me.

WILLIAM HAMILTON: The L.A.W. has added a color bar to their constitution, which means I want nothing to do with them. That's my statement.

BENZINA: You attend local L.A.W. meets.

WILLIAM HAMILTON: Not the national. We have protested at the Charles Street Meeting House. If the L.A.W. is willing to treat us like trash just to court Southern riders, I don't need to be a part of their extravaganza.

ROBERT TEAMOH: My measure condemning the L.A.W. was passed by my fellow lawmakers in the State House. The L.A.W. will never admit me to the meet.

KITTIE: I've been a member since I was sixteen years old. I pay my dues every year.

VIOLA HAMILTON: What if they pretend not to know you?

KITTIE: I have my membership ticket, paid for with my own money.

BENZINA: *(to Teamoh)* You could go. You're a politician and a journalist. We need a Colored reporter there to write the truth.

VIOLA HAMILTON: Leave him be.

WILLIAM HAMILTON: *(to Teamoh)* It could be an opportunity.

KITTIE: It will be fun.

ROBERT TEAMOH: Is that what you think?

BENZINA: I'm sure New Jersey won't be anything like Virginia.

ROBERT TEAMOH: That's right. In Virginia, I was on an official trade mission, and I had a whole group of White lawmakers beside me. In New Jersey, it would just be me, Robert Teamoh, Colored cyclist.

BENZINA: Other Massachusetts riders will be there, like Mr. Bassett and Mr. Percival.

KITTIE: And me.

ROBERT TEAMOH: When the Virginia governor refused to admit our delegation to the Capitol unless I remained outside on the steps, did the White Massachusetts delegates suddenly grow spines and shun the meeting?

WILLIAM HAMILTON: They did not.

ROBERT TEAMOH: Do you imagine the White cyclists from Cambridge and Boston are more principled than their lawmakers?

KITTIE: They might be.

ROBERT TEAMOH: And when I returned home, my dark-skinned constituents denounced me as a coward because I did not spit in the face of a Southern Governor and end up dangling from a rope.

KITTIE: You were treated unfairly both there and here.

ROBERT TEAMOH: You don't need to subject yourself to it.

WILLIAM HAMILTON: Surely you got enough attention from the Waltham costume competition.

VIOLA HAMILTON: Hush, William!

WILLIAM HAMILTON: All eyes will be watching her in New Jersey. And they will not be kind.

ROBERT TEAMOH: Have you at least written to the Asbury Park Colored ministers for support? If you're going to stage a protest, do it with help.

WILLIAM HAMILTON: Reverend Robinson tried to integrate the beaches there with "wade ins" a few years ago. But failed.

KITTIE: I'm not going to protest; I'm going to ride.

ROBERT TEAMOH: Your pretty smile and charm work well in Boston. Don't expect them to be effective farther South.

BENZINA: It's only New Jersey.

ROBERT TEAMOH: The South extends farther north than you realize.

Joshua Lee Robinson, Rebekah Brunson

KITTIE: So, none of you think I should go?

ROBERT TEAMOH: Absolutely not.

WILLIAM HAMILTON: They're not worth your time.

VIOLA HAMILTON: It's dangerous.

BENZINA: I don't know.

KITTIE: Benzina?

BENZINA: You know I'm always on your side, Kittie. But.

KITTIE: Tell the office that you're sick. Or it's a family emergency. There will be cycling. We'll scorch along the seaside. There will be salt-water taffy and waves and nights of music and dancing.

BENZINA: I can't.

ROBERT TEAMOH: And you shouldn't.

WILLIAM HAMILTON: No one will think less of you for not going, Kittie.

BENZINA: But they will think more of you if you do.

VIOLA HAMILTON: Don't encourage her.

BENZINA: Miss Kittie Knox is a woman of strong spirit; if eyes will be watching her, then good.

KITTIE: I am not going there to be seen.

VIOLA HAMILTON: Oh, honey, with that outfit, you will be noticed.

KITTIE: It's practical. Now, the ball gown I've sewn, that is just for show.

WILLIAM HAMILTON: If you go, avoid the Louisville club and their leader, Colonel Watts. They will be foaming at the mouth at the sight of you on a bike, and they won't know what to do once you start gliding across the dance floor.

KITTIE: Maybe you could bring the entire Riverside Cycling Club to Asbury Park and show them our best stuff? Bring some lawyers, too.

ROBERT TEAMOH: The law isn't always on our side. It is here in Massachusetts, for the moment—

WILLIAM HAMILTON: Thanks to your accommodation law.

ROBERT TEAMOH: But there are cases before the Supreme Court right now that might make things much worse.

WILLIAM HAMILTON: Going as a club would take planning and fundraising. Committees.

KITTIE: I don't need a committee to give me permission to live my life. They can join me if they want.

VIOLA HAMILTON: Don't worry, they're not going. I like my man in one piece.

WILLIAM HAMILTON: *(to Kittie)* And we want you to be in one piece, too.

KITTIE: I'm from the West End. I know how to take care of myself.

ROBERT TEAMOH: This is not a game, Miss Knox.

KITTIE: Yes, it is. I'm going to ride with thousands of other people, joined together by our love of the wind in our faces and the whir of the gears. Which feels like the smartest, safest, most joyful thing in the world.

ROBERT TEAMOH: Joining together is exactly what they're afraid of.

KITTIE: Black and White people can love each other. I'm living proof—I have a Black father from Philadelphia and a White mother from Maine.

BENZINA: You should go show them.

KITTIE: I will.

(Kittie gets on her bike and rides.)

ROBERT TEAMOH: There is no reasoning with that woman.

BENZINA: That's why I love her.

(They all pack up and start riding.)

Tom Berry

Scene 2

>   *(Viola and William Hamilton ride out of view, but Teamoh and Benzina stick around.)*
>
>   *(Kittie rides back into the scene and eventually stopping in front of the audience.)*

BENZINA: *(to audience)* It's a two-day trip from Boston to Asbury Park.

ROBERT TEAMOH: *(to audience)* She's not the only cyclist on her way to the L.A.W. meet.

>   *(Charley Percival, Abbot Bassett, and Mary Sargent Hopkins ride into our view. Abbot and Mary keep riding until they are out of sight. Charley stops near Kittie.)*

BENZINA: *(to audience)* Kittie takes the train from Boston to Providence.

ROBERT TEAMOH: *(to audience)* Charley Percival is on that train, too, part of a group from the Boston Press Cycling Club. The cars are crowded with riders and their bikes.

(Charley waves to catch Kittie's attention, but she's focused on her own progress. He positions his bike next to Kittie.)

BENZINA: *(to audience)* The train connects them with an overnight boat that joins a flotilla of overnight passenger ships and freighters and barges steaming across the Long Island Sound to New York.

(Kittie and Charley sway their bikes as if rocking on the deck of a ship.)

BENZINA: *(to audience)* Kittie and Charley meet on the deck of the *Priscilla* as it steams through the night.

CHARLEY PERCIVAL: Miss Knox? I am surprised to see you here. Are you on your way to Asbury Park?

KITTIE: I am.

CHARLEY PERCIVAL: I am confident you will make an impressive showing there, just like you did in Waltham. Congratulations on your win.

KITTIE: I suppose I have you to thank for that.

CHARLEY PERCIVAL: Your costume was clearly the most fashionable and well-constructed. It was an easy decision for us judges.

KITTIE: It was not a universally popular choice.

CHARLEY PERCIVAL: Those women hissing were just jealous. And perhaps a bit fearful of bloomers. It's never possible to make everyone happy. Are you excited about New Jersey?

KITTIE: Yes. Though I might have some trepidation.

CHARLEY PERCIVAL: I'm sure it will be fine. *(beat)* What a night! The lights on the ships and stars on the water.

KITTIE: Like we're floating on an infinite sky.

(They sway a bit more and admire the skies and sea.)

ROBERT TEAMOH: *(to audience)* The next morning, they arrive at Pier 18 in New York and hustle to board a train heading south on the Central Railroad of New Jersey.

(Kittie and Charley shift their bikes, no longer on a ship. A train whistle blows.)

BENZINA: *(to audience)* Which takes them to Asbury Park, on Monday, July 8, 1895.

Scene 3

The L.A.W. meet in Asbury Park, NJ.

(Charley gives a wave and rides away. Kittie mounts her bike warily but brightens once she's riding. A long loop, as two people (Gertrude and Mary) bring on a small wooden table with a banner that reads "League of American Wheelmen Annual Meet. 1895. Registration."; Teamoh and Benzina watch from the edge of the performing area.)

(The check-in staffer, Gertrude Parker, sets up behind the Registration table. She's a young, friendly, White woman.)

(Charley Percival cycles to the Registration table. He's all smiles and is a natural flirt. Kittie continues riding, in the distance.)

CHARLEY PERCIVAL: Good afternoon, Miss?

GERTUDE: Parker. Welcome to Asbury Park and the National Meet.

CHARLEY PERCIVAL: It's a wondrous day. So many cyclists! What a place! The seaside, the boardwalk, so many lovely sights! Even right here. *(with a wink at her)*

GERTUDE: Let me check you in. Your name?

CHARLEY PERCIVAL: Percival. Charles Percival. I'm the cycling editor for the *Boston Daily Journal.*

GERTUDE: Are you here to write or to ride?

CHARLEY PERCIVAL: Both. Are you a rider? You have such a healthy glow, surely you're a cyclist.

GERTUDE: I do like to ride. We have a ladies club here in Asbury Park. I see your name on the list, Mr. Percival. Here is your badge for the meet, which will get you access to all the scheduled rides, the balls, and is good for one free bathing suit rental, plus a ticket to the Crystal Maze at the Palace and a free spin at the Wheel of Fortune. You'll find a printed map of the town and a schedule for the week.

(She hands him a little bag of swag.)

CHARLEY PERCIVAL: Thank you, Miss Parker. I hope they don't keep you chained to this desk all week.

GERTUDE: I'm sure I'll get some time away.

CHARLEY PERCIVAL: Perhaps we will see you on a ride. Or at one of the dances?

GERTUDE: Perhaps you will. Have a lovely week, Mr. Percival. Who's next?

(Charley rides off.)

(Kittie might do a fancy trick as she rides past the table. Finally, she works up her nerve and approaches.)

KITTIE: I'm here to register for the meet.

GERTUDE: I think you're in the wrong place.

KITTIE: This is the registration table for The League of American Wheelmen's Annual Meet, isn't it? I need my badge.

GERTUDE: The meet badges are for L.A.W. members only.

(She produces her membership card.)

KITTIE: My dues are fully paid. Here's my membership card.

GERTUDE: There must be some mistake.

KITTIE: I paid my fee for the meet months ago. Here's my receipt.

(She produces her receipt.)

GERTUDE: But that's not possible.

KITTIE: You have a list of registered attendees, don't you? Look up my name. Knox. K. For Kittie. Short for Katherine, but that's also my mom's name, so she gets to be Kate and I'm Kittie. Under K. K-N-O-X. Right there. K. Knox.

GERTUDE: But the . . . I was told that last year, they changed the League constitution, so that only White people could become members.

KITTIE: Oh, they did. But I was already a member. I've been a member since I was sixteen years old. I love to ride. I love the wind in my face, the sound of the tires on the road, the way the world speeds up and slows down all once.

GERTUDE: But. But. But.

(Gertrude rings a small bell to call for help. If she has a bike next to her, maybe it's her bicycle bell.)

KITTIE: So, if you can just give me my badge and the associated little bag of maps and treats, I will be on my way and check into my hotel.

GERTUDE: You won't find a hotel room in Asbury Park.

KITTIE: Let's deal with one obstacle at a time, shall we?

GERTUDE: If you walk west down Springwood Street, you might find a place that will take your kind.

KITTIE: My "kind" is a cyclist, and I'd like my badge, please.

GERTUDE: You might find a room in a cottage. Look for the signs. The larger, nicer places will say "Whites Only"; so obviously don't try those.

KITTIE: And the not-so-nice places? What do their signs say?

GERTUDE: "Equal Rights."

KITTIE: Do you notice a problem with that?

GERTUDE: Miss.

KITTIE: Knox. Kittie Knox. Like it says on the registration list in front of you. Like it says on my membership card. Like it says on my receipt.

GERTUDE: Kittie. I would like to help you. But I don't know how.

KITTIE: You haven't encountered this problem yet today?

GERTUDE: You're the first. Um.

KITTIE: Problem? Today?

GERTUDE: To attempt to register. Yes.

(Gertrude frantically rings her bell.)

KITTIE: Do you really think that is going to help?

GERTUDE: Someone will help me.

KITTIE: What's your name?

GERTUDE: Excuse me.

KITTIE: What is your name, Miss?

GERTUDE: Parker. Gertrude Parker.

KITTIE: Miss Parker, I'm not going anywhere until I get my badge.

GERTUDE: I can't give it to you. Other people will tell me what to do.

KITTIE: All you're going to do is attract a crowd. People are watching us. I don't think that's what anyone wants.

(Mary Sargent Hopkins rides onto the scene, stares at the commotion disapprovingly, and rides away.)

GERTUDE: I certainly don't want a commotion, but—

KITTIE: Give me my badge, Gertrude!

(The action freezes for a moment. Teamoh and Benzina approach the audience.)

ROBERT TEAMOH: *(to audience)* This is where the historical record gets fuzzy. Which is a shock considering how many cycling reporters attended the meet.

BENZINA: *(to audience)* If a Black journalist had been there, he might have reported on it accurately.

ROBERT TEAMOH: Let it go, Benzina. *(to audience)* Colonel William Watts of Kentucky was at the meet. Perhaps he rushed to the aid of the beleaguered desk worker.

(Charley Percival rides onto the scene. Benzina gives him a Southerner's white jacket and hat, and Charley reluctantly becomes Colonel Watts.)

COLONEL WATTS: I am Colonel Watts, from Louisville. What seems to be the problem here, young lady?

GERTUDE: This young. Negro. Says she has a badge waiting for her and that she should be allowed entrance to the meet.

COLONEL WATTS: Did you give it to her?

GERTUDE: Not yet. I'm confused about the rules.

COLONEL WATTS: There is no confusion. We amended the by-laws to solve this exact problem. The League of American Wheelmen is for White riders. Respectable Southern Gentlemen cannot be expected to participate in activities that permit racial mixing. It turns my stomach to even think of it. This is why Asbury Park is such a perfect location for the meet. Your lovely little town understands there is an order to the world.

(Abbot Bassett rides onto the scene.)

Dustin Teuber, Em Sheeran, Tom Berry, Hampton Richards

COLONEL WATTS: Secretary Bassett. There is no need to concern yourself with this matter. We have it under control.

ABBOT BASSETT: Mr. Watts, as Secretary of the League, everything here is my concern. *(to Kittie)* Hello, Kittie.

KITTIE: Mr. Bassett, it is always a pleasure to see you.

COLONEL WATTS: It's Colonel Watts.

ABBOT BASSETT: A "Colonel" in the Kentucky militia. I'm sure that title gives you a certain cachet in your local papers, but we're not in Kentucky.

COLONEL WATTS: You lost the vote, Mr. Bassett. You need to accept that.

ABBOT BASSETT: In your campaign for the color bar, I seem to recall a promise of five thousand new Southern members once the danger of associating with Colored riders was removed. I've combed the membership rolls, but those new cyclists are nowhere to be found.

COLONEL WATTS: Be that as it may, the rules state clearly—

ABBOT BASSETT: That new members must be White. But it doesn't say anything about previous members.

KITTIE: That's what I was trying to tell her.

COLONEL WATTS: But the intent was clearly—

ABBOT BASSETT: You're a lawyer. There is intent and then there is the clarity of the written language.

COLONEL WATTS: It was assumed that once the message was clear that they are not welcome, the Colored cyclists would not choose to ride.

KITTIE: I intend to ride. Whether you want me here or not.

ABBOT BASSETT: We have lawyers on our side, too, Mr. Watts.

COLONEL WATTS: Colonel.

ABBOT BASSETT: Our League Vice President, Mr. Perkins, is a highly skilled attorney, and I promise he will reduce your defense to dust. I can send for him.

COLONEL WATTS: That won't be necessary.

ABBOT BASSETT: What will be necessary is for this young registrar to give Miss Knox her badge and allow her to enjoy the meet like the rest of the members.

COLONEL WATTS: This is why we didn't hold the meet in Boston.

ABBOT BASSETT: I can see why you would not feel welcome there. And, unlike Miss Knox, you chose to stay away. You've gotten most of what you wanted, perhaps you could be satisfied with that.

(to Kittie) Miss Knox, there is a ride tomorrow to the home of former racing champion Arthur Zimmerman. I hope you will join us.

KITTIE: I'm a big fan of Mr. Zimmerman!

ABBOT BASSETT: It will be a fast ride and they need pacesetters. I know you have a talent for speed.

KITTIE: Thank you, Mr. Bassett.

ABBOT BASSETT: Oh, Watts. You're still here. Don't let us keep you.

(Watts rides off in a huff. At the edge of our view, the actor stops and discards the jacket and hat and puts on his Charley Percival costume again. Then rides off.)

ABBOT BASSETT: *(to Kittie)* I hope you enjoy your stay, as best you can.

(Bassett rides off.)

(Kittie stands in front of Gertrude, waiting. Not to be moved.)

BENZINA: *(to audience)* The incident is reported in dozens of papers.

ROBERT TEAMOH: *(to audience)* Few agree on the details. Was Colonel Watts the villain? Did anyone stand up for Kittie?

BENZINA: *(to audience)* I'm not sure Kittie needed anyone to rescue her.

ROBERT TEAMOH: *(to audience)* She was one of the only women mentioned in any reporting about the meet.

BENZINA: *(to audience)* Whichever version of that day is true, one thing we know: Kittie rides.

(Teamoh and Benzina ride off.)

KITTIE: I'd like my badge please.

GERTUDE: But.

KITTIE: No one is coming to rescue you. And I'm not leaving until I get it.

GERTUDE: I'm just a volunteer. They said it would be fun.

KITTIE: It can be. Just get out of my way and let me ride. No one will ever know your name.

(Gertrude thinks it over and checks off Kittie's name and hands her a badge and the swag bag.)

(Kittie pins the badge on her dress and gets on her bike. Maybe does a trick in front of the registration table.)

(Charley Percival rides into the scene, fast.)

CHARLEY PERCIVAL: We're on a fast ride to Long Branch, Miss Knox. Join us!

KITTIE: I'm with you!

(Together, they speed off out of sight.)

(Gertrude packs up the table and exits.)

— End of Play —

THE

Ball

by Claire Soleil Gardner

Characters

Viola Hamilton (died)

Benzina Reese

Kittie Knox

William Hamilton

Robert Teamoh

John J. Walsh

Ethel Armitadge Walsh

Fred St. Onge

Mary Sargent Hopkins

Scene 1

> *April 1896. Boston.*
>
> *(Viola Hamilton rides in.)*

VIOLA HAMILTON: A year has passed since the summer Kittie arrived in Asbury Park. Doesn't summer always go by too fast? We always think we have more time. Summer turned to fall, too soon. That fall I slowly noticed a pain in my stomach, on my right side. I dismissed William's worries, I'm tougher than look, and there's no way I was willingly going to a hospital. Then, the pain got worse, far too quickly. At first, the doctors thought it might be a good sign. A sign of a baby. Everything changed when the doctor said, "acute appendicitis." Strange men in strange masks took me away from my husband. I never saw him again. I never got to tease Kittie's mannish bloomers with Benzina again. I never got to prove to Kittie that she doesn't know everything. Now I know something I hope she never will. I know what it's like to die too young. Everyone talks about the grief of the living, but what about my grief? I know it's selfish to be lonely. I don't want anyone else to die. But I hope one day I'll have my husband and my friends by my side again. Now, they must go on living the best they can without me.

> *(Kittie rides in and takes from her basket a dress. She uses the wheel of her bike as a sewing machine. The sounds of the sewing machine come to life.)*
>
> *(Viola hesitates, briefly looking at Kittie, before riding away.)*
>
> *(Benzina Reese enters.)*

BENZINA: Hey Kittie, you ready to go? Still sewing?

KITTIE: Until my fingers go numb. Gotta sew a lot more dresses before I can buy myself a new bike. Do you like it?

BENZINA: I love it.

KITTIE: Good. It'll get me through tonight.

BENZINA: This dress is for you? And you didn't make a matching one for me?!

KITTIE: I'm going out dancing tonight. I've been invited to the Consolidated Cycle Club's ball.

BENZINA: Kittie! We're having dinner tonight, remember? You agreed to come with me to take William Hamilton out, and I invited Robert Teamoh, too.

KITTIE: I completely forgot. Next time?

BENZINA: I don't know if I can handle a next time, cheering up these grumpy old men.

KITTIE: You're not being very convincing, Benzina.

BENZINA: Please come Kittie. You said you would.

KITTIE: I didn't realize it was the same night as the ball. I'm sorry.

BENZINA: I don't know of anyone else invited to this ball. You'll probably be the only Colored person there.

KITTIE: You can't know that for sure.

BENZINA: Do you really think they've invited anyone from Riverside? Or any of the Colored cycling groups?

(William Hamilton, still in mourning, enters trailed by Robert Teamoh.)

ROBERT TEAMOH: Are you ladies ready to get something to eat?

WILLIAM HAMILTON: What's this about Riverside?

BENZINA: Kittie's ditching our dinner to go to a League ball.

WILLIAM HAMILTON: Let me get this right. Instead of spending time with your friends, you'd rather dance with the supporters of the color bar?

KITTIE: It's just a ball. Please don't lecture me, it makes you seem even older than you are.

WILLIAM HAMILTON: If you go to this ball you'll be used as a political prop, is that what you want?

KITTIE: No! But you don't even know the people at this ball.

ROBERT TEAMOH: Kittie, I don't think you should go either.

KITTIE: Do you think I'm just a helpless prop, too? I can take care of myself.

WILLIAM HAMILTON: Tell her about that Supreme Court case you told me about.

ROBERT TEAMOH: It's called Plessy v. Ferguson. Homer Plessy was a mixed-race man who boarded a Whites-only train to protest the Louisiana Separate Car Act. Because of his protest, the Supreme Court will hear arguments on whether the segregation of public accommodations is legal. If he wins, it will be a huge victory. But if he loses, then there's precedent that segregation is constitutional and can be implemented everywhere, even here.

KITTIE: There's no way it's constitutional. It's clearly discrimination.

BENZINA: Kittie, it's bad that they're even hearing it.

ROBERT TEAMOH: If they rule segregation is constitutional, we will be unable to go anywhere unless it's marked explicitly for Colored people. And we know what kind of places the White people will want to keep us in.

KITTIE: And what will they do about people like me? Separate the White and Colored that's already mixed inside me? Or in Homer Plessy? I'm about to go to a ball with White people. Or did they only invite the White part of me, and expect the rest to be left at the door?

ROBERT TEAMOH: I think if they could only invite the White part of you, they would.

WILLIAM HAMILTON: Mhm.

KITTIE: Enough. Tonight is about lifting our spirits, something Robert's depressing legal jargon will not help with.

ROBERT TEAMOH: But Kittie, listen, one Supreme Court ruling could change our lives—

BENZINA: We should go to dinner. Mr. Hamilton, Mr. Teamoh, I'll meet you outside, I need to talk to Kittie.

(Robert Teamoh exits.)

WILLIAM HAMILTON: Enjoy your ball, Miss Knox. I hope breaking your word to a man in mourning is worth it.

KITTIE: It's not like that!

(William Hamilton exits.)

You know it's not like that.

BENZINA: I know. Don't you wish Viola was here? She'd know how to argue with the boys.

KITTIE: I wish she was here more than anything.

BENZINA: William is heartbroken too. That's why he's—

KITTIE: He doesn't have the right to take it out on me!

BENZINA: You don't have the right to take it out on him either! Try to be more understanding. He lost a wife.

KITTIE: She was more than his wife!

BENZINA: I know.

KITTIE: We're mourning, too.

I need to go. I'm going to be late.

BENZINA: Just promise me you'll turn right around if anything goes wrong?

KITTIE: I'll be fine. You don't need to mother me.

BENZINA: With Viola gone, I do. Be careful.

(Benzina exits. There is "bikeography" as Kittie rides away towards the ball. Music begins.)

Beyoncé Martinez

Scene 2

April 1896. The ball at Boston Music Hall.

(Music plays.)

(The ball guests ride in, including the Walshes, Mary Sargent Hopkins, and Fred St. Onge. Kittie enters in her batiste and blue silk gown with Dresden trimmings.)

(They form a gathering and enjoy the concert. The concert comes to a close and they applaud the musicians.)

(Floor director, John J. Walsh, accompanied by his wife, Mrs. Ethel Armitadge Walsh, address the group assembled for the ball.)

JOHN J. WALSH: Let's all give another round of applause to the band for that wonderful concert.

(Ball attendees applaud and if there are live musicians they bow.)

JOHN J. WALSH: I am John J. Walsh, President of the Malden Bicycle Club. My lovely wife, Mrs. Ethel Armitadge Walsh, and I will be your floor directors for this evening. I'd like to formally welcome you to the first Consolidated Cycling Club ball of 1896! Let the dancing begin!

(Music resumes. Two couples, the Walshes, Mary Sargent Hopkins, and Fred St. Onge enter the dance floor. Their "bikeography" begins. They make passes across the space on their bikes, switching positions with each other in tune with the music. Kittie watches, feeling left out. The Walshes remain and Mary and Fred exit.)

(Kittie walks towards the Walshes.)

KITTIE: Hello and good evening. Where might I find a partner and join?

MRS. WALSH: That is not an introduction.

KITTIE: I see. I am Miss Katherine—

JOHN J. WALSH: My god! It must be Miss Kittie Knox, correct?

KITTIE: Yes, it is.

MRS. WALSH: Who?

JOHN J. WALSH: A cycling sensation in the flesh! You may also know her as the Beanville Goddess.

Tom Berry, Em Sheeran, Jen Drummond

She's been in all the papers for her exploits, she's what we cyclists call a scorcher. Miss Knox, you must save me a spot on your dance card so I may pick your brain about your adventures.

KITTIE: I'd be happy to.

MRS. WALSH: I'm sure you could discuss scorching without dancing together, darling.

JOHN J. WALSH: I suspect I'll have to once word gets around to our club members that Kittie Knox has made an appearance. Your dance card is sure to fill up quickly. Please, join the waltz.

KITTIE: I'm not sure about all of that, but thank you very much, Mr. Walsh and Mrs. Walsh.

(Kittie walks to the dance floor, where a nervous, young White male rider, Fred St. Onge, offers her a bike.)

FRED ST. ONGE: Uh, Miss Kittie Knox? Would you, um, care for a dance?

KITTIE: I see my reputation precedes me. And you are?

FRED ST. ONGE: Nobody really, compared to you.

KITTIE: I'm sure that can't be true. I recognize you. I think I've seen you down by the Reservoir, right?

FRED ST. ONGE: I'm often there. I like to race.

KITTIE: You're Fred St. Onge, aren't you? You're more than a racer; you're a trick rider. I've seen you stand on your bicycle seat and somehow balance. I wish you would teach me how to do that! And you've done a vaudeville circuit or two, haven't you?

FRED ST. ONGE: Forgive my bad manners, I should've led with my name. I—I just didn't know exactly what to say when I realized it was you. I've only ever heard other club members describe the effect your beauty can have, but in person, it's entirely different, beyond human description. You are what a man's dreams are made of, Kittie Knox!

KITTIE: You're not so bad yourself. I'd like to learn some of your tricks, maybe even take to the stage. Would you show me some time?

FRED ST. ONGE: I'm sure you would take to them quickly. You ride like you could do anything at all.

KITTIE: Next time we're both at the Reservoir, let's find out.

FRED ST. ONGE: Really? Oh, Ms. Knox, you must come ride with me, or else my friends will never believe I danced with you!

KITTIE: Are you sure they won't be scandalized by my person? Or by my person mixing with yours?

FRED ST. ONGE: By your person? Do you mean because you're Colored? Ms. Knox, I hope Boston men have treated you better than that. Whatever the League thinks, you will always have the boys of Boston behind you. I think the color bar is wholly ridiculous, and if anyone takes issue with our dancing together I will give them a taste of my fisticuffs—

KITTIE: Show me how the Boston boys dance, instead of fight, alright?

(They begin riding together doing the same "bikeography" as done in the beginning. Mrs. Walsh and Mr. Walsh observe them.)

MRS. WALSH: John, she shouldn't be dancing with any of the club members if she hasn't been properly introduced by a chaperone.

JOHN J. WALSH: Her reputation is her chaperone. Dear, you wouldn't understand. In the world of cycling, she's a goddess.

MRS. WALSH: Goddess or not, it is improper for a single young lady to introduce herself to men without a chaperone. She did not seek my permission to dance with you either. Her appearance will cast an improper shadow on the ball.

JOHN J. WALSH: Ethel, if the ball is too proper it won't be any fun. We must think of the young members. Besides, the extra press we are sure to get from her appearance won't hurt our cause either.

MRS. WALSH: What about the politics of having someone like her dancing with White partners?

JOHN J. WALSH: Leave the politics to me. It's a man's pursuit, and as you are a lady, it would be improper to worry yourself so much about it. Ah! I see a worry line between your brows darling. How improper!

(As Kittie and her current partner, Fred St. Onge, finish their exchange, they dismount. Mr. Walsh cuts in.)

JOHN J. WALSH: Miss Knox. May I have the next dance?

FRED ST. ONGE: But—

KITTIE: It's alright, Fred. I promised Mr. Walsh a dance.

JOHN J. WALSH: I've read so much about you in the papers, Miss Knox. I'm looking forward to getting the inside scoop.

KITTIE: You may have to keep looking. Shall we?

(Fred gives John his bike. They mount their bikes and ride with the music, despite a heartbroken Fred St. Onge.)

(While they ride, Mary Sargent Hopkins approaches Mrs. Walsh.)

MARY SARGENT HOPKINS: Hello, dear. I don't think we've been introduced yet. I am Mrs. Mary Sargent Hopkins.

MRS. WALSH: What a pleasure to make your acquaintance.

MARY SARGENT HOPKINS: I publish the women's cycling paper, *The Wheelwoman.* You may know my writing under the name Merrie Wheeler.

MRS. WALSH: Oh, my goodness, I'm such a fan of your magazine! I am Mrs. John J. Walsh. Welcome to the ball. My husband and I are the floor directors this evening.

MARY SARGENT HOPKINS: Dear, your husband is on the floor, and not directing it.

MRS. WALSH: Yes, he was too excited by the presence of this Kittie person. I'm unsure how she was invited to an event such as this given her... background.

MARY SARGENT HOPKINS: I am familiar with the exploits of Miss Kittie Knox. Cycling men from all over know her name.

MRS. WALSH: Is she often unchaperoned with married men?

MARY SARGENT HOPKINS: What do you think, dear? She has a flirtatious air, with practically every man, married or not...

MRS. WALSH: I need my John away from her now! With her temptations and impudence to manners. Her kind clearly can't be trusted around proper ladies' husbands. She shouldn't be here in the first place.

MARY SARGENT HOPKINS: But we cannot storm the dance floor and separate her from your husband, can we?

MRS. WALSH: No, we can't. What a horrible shadow she is casting on my ball!

MARY SARGENT HOPKINS: And with your husband no doubt. Oh, dear.

(The song ends, and Kittie says goodbye to Mr. Walsh. She resumes the dance/bikeography to the next song with Fred St. Onge.)

MRS. WALSH: And now she already has a partner again! If only we could get her off the floor.

(Mr. John J. Walsh approaches the ladies.)

JOHN J. WALSH: Enjoying the festivities, ladies? Good to see you here, Mrs. Hopkins. I need to find myself a refreshment, I leave the rest of the dancing for the young people tonight!

MARY SARGENT HOPKINS: Surely, you'll save at least one last dance for your lovely wife? You can't let your last dance of the night be with . . . her.

JOHN J. WALSH: Oh, darling Ethel would never accept even if I offered. I'm lucky she danced with me at all.

MRS. WALSH: I can't believe you danced with another woman, and a Negress at that! It is completely improper and because of the precedent you set she will be dancing with White partners all night!

JOHN J. WALSH: This is Kittie Knox, she would be danced with whether or not I did anything. Many of these young men are League members against the color bar. Whether it's her looks or their politics, she'll dance.

MARY SARGENT HOPKINS: Perhaps that is the problem. Mr. Walsh, as floor director, could you take Miss Knox off the floor so we could inform her of the proper etiquette before more ladies get offended?

JOHN J. WALSH: Kittie Knox has a right to be here.

(The music stops. Kittie stops riding/dancing. She overhears.)

MARY SARGENT HOPKINS: Honestly, dear, this is just a disaster. I may have to bring this situation up in my magazine.

JOHN J. WALSH: Mrs. Hopkins, there's no need.

MRS. WALSH: You wouldn't mention that it was our ball? It would be so terrible for the cycling clubs if you did.

MARY SARGENT HOPKINS: I don't have to mention the ball, dear. Especially if your husband were to ask her to leave.

JOHN J. WALSH: I will do no such thing. She was invited; she has a right to keep dancing.

MRS. WALSH: John!

MARY SARGENT HOPKINS: And I have a right to publish.

MRS. WALSH: John, do something!

JOHN J. WALSH: I will. I'm going to go get something to drink. Would you like anything?

MRS. WALSH: Yes! I'd like you to remove—

JOHN J. WALSH: No. Don't nag me, Ethel.

MRS. WALSH: Please, Mrs. Sargent Hopkins, don't publish anything about the ball.

MARY SARGENT HOPKINS: Don't worry about your ball, dear. I'll only say that the whole affair was a bit of misplaced and misguided chivalry of a few youths, who seem to think the young woman was entitled to more than her share of courtesy; thus, making a sensation, about the young woman, who evidently was not at all adverse to her notoriety.

MRS. WALSH: You'll make sure not to cast a shadow on the ball?

MARY SARGENT HOPKINS: The shadow has been dancing at your ball all night, dear.

(Kittie steps out of the scene to address the audience.)

KITTIE: I was having such a lovely night. Until now. Maybe I should just leave, run right out those doors and let them slam behind me. No, I don't run away from anything. But my friends were right. Maybe I shouldn't have come in the first place. I wish Benzina was here. I wish I wasn't alone. The only Colored woman in a sea of White faces.

(Benzina enters.)

BENZINA: If I was here and I did have some advice, would you even listen to me?

KITTIE: If there's one thing I've learned tonight, it is to always listen to you.

BENZINA: You really want to know what I think of all this?

KITTIE: Of course I do.

BENZINA: I think there's prejudiced people in cycling. Even in Boston. You promised you'd turn around if—

KITTIE: I know, but should I let them run me out of the room with petty gossip? Wouldn't that be letting them win?

BENZINA: You asked what I think. Please, try not to interrupt. I think your safety is more important—

KITTIE: What danger am I in?

BENZINA: Kittie! You can be so naive! Not to mention stubborn!

KITTIE: I'm sorry. I know I asked, but . . . You know me. I can't let them win. I'm staying.

BENZINA: You really want to listen to this? Because I've heard enough.

KITTIE: Please stay with me. I can't do this alone.

(Benzina sighs and takes Kittie's hand and stays with her. Kittie continues to eavesdrop, now joined by Benzina.)

JOHN J. WALSH: She was just dancing. Isn't that what she's supposed to do at a ball?

MRS. WALSH: Of course, she can dance, but a lady must have—

(Mary Sargent Hopkins begins to stiffly walk regally.)

MARY SARGENT HOPKINS: An easy, becoming, and graceful movement while dancing or walking because it's more pleasing to the gentleman. A lady must never—

(Mary Sargent Hopkins starts correcting Mrs. Walsh's posture.)

MRS. WALSH: Dance with a man she hasn't been properly introduced to, and a lady should not attend a ball without an escort or promenade the ballroom alone. And—

(Mrs. Walsh and Mary Sargent Hopkins continue correcting each other's form.)

MARY SARGENT HOPKINS: Ladies should not be too eager to fill up their dance card. It shows a want for refinement. And—

KITTIE: And they should not be Colored ladies.

(Mrs. Walsh and Mary Sargent Hopkins stop still.)

MARY SARGENT HOPKINS: Well, I didn't say that, dear.

KITTIE: You would just publish it if someone else said it for you.

MARY SARGENT HOPKINS: Who's gossiping now, dear?

KITTIE: All these ladylike confinements ruin all the freedom you get from dancing. If that's what it takes to be a ladylike dancer or rider, count me out.

MARY SARGENT HOPKINS: Don't worry, I've already counted you out from ladylike cycling.

KITTIE: Where has being so ladylike gotten you? You've never been allowed to race in any League meets. You still publish your magazine under a fake name.

MARY SARGENT HOPKINS: I have fostered a future for women cyclists of every color. You should be thanking me for all I've done. Just because I will not slow down progress by indulging every problem of the Colored, does not mean I have not contributed to the privileges you enjoy.

KITTIE: I don't need you to save me. The least you can do is get out of my way and stop publishing prejudiced lies.

MARY SARGENT HOPKINS: I run a magazine. I publish what I want. Is that a crime?

KITTIE: Publishing lies should be a crime.

MARY SARGENT HOPKINS: Good luck with that, dear.

(Mary Sargent Hopkins exits, and the other members of the previous ball begin to exit.)

KITTIE: I don't want this ridiculous drama to ruin my night. They're going to talk about me no matter what I do. I might as well dance while they're at it.

BENZINA: You'll dance the whole rest of the night with a full dance card, just to show them you can.

KITTIE: I can't let them think I'm afraid of them. That's not my story. Everything they said in the papers, that's not my story either. I'm not a goddess; I have plenty of flaws that need forgiving.

BENZINA: Forgiveness is what friends are for.

KITTIE: Benzina, what will my story be, if all that's left is what was said and printed behind my back?

BENZINA: Your friends know your story.

(Robert Teamoh enters.)

ROBERT TEAMOH: We know you have a great one to tell. I've never let what they printed about me define me. But I know how it stings. If we are telling your story, we need to tell the story of Kittie Knox, with all the vibrant joy you bring into the West End and all of Boston.

BENZINA: We weren't welcome at the CCC ball. But we can have our own ball tonight.

KITTIE: But who will we dance with?

Nathan Johnson, Joshua Lee Robinson, Hampton Richards, Rebekah Brunson

WILLIAM HAMILTON: I'll dance. I can even try to keep up with you, Kittie, despite my age.

(They take up bikes and take to the floor. Lively music starts up and they ride. Benzina and Teamoh join in.)

BENZINA: Kittie, show us what you've got!

(Kittie rides away and comes speeding back.)

KITTIE: Good enough for you, Benzina?

BENZINA: You always look so happy when you ride. So free.

(Kittie stops riding.)

KITTIE: Of course I'm happy. What's better than freedom?

(Kittie dismounts. Her friends get back on their bikes and slowly circle her.)

KITTIE: Freedom. The wind in my hair and the heat in my cheeks. Pumping my legs and getting faster, and faster until I'm flying. I can fly away from the noise and smell of Boston, away from hours at a sewing machine. I can look up and see the sparkling golden light coming down through the leaves of the trees above me. Feel its warmth on my face.

One day, I will look ahead and be on the racetrack. I won't just scorch, I'll race, and I'll win. One day, women will be free to ride as we please, wearing whatever we please, voting for whoever we please. One day, I won't be the only Colored woman in the building. I know I'll see this all in my lifetime. We're less than five years from the twentieth century. Things may be dark now, but they are always darkest before the dawn. I can't wait to cycle for the rest of my life. If you see a little old lady with white hair speed past you on a bike, in Martha's Vineyard, or Cambridge, or Boston, you'll know it was me. And I was so incredibly happy.

(Viola cycles in and sets her bike next to Kittie.)

KITTIE: Viola?

VIOLA: I've been waiting for you. I could've waited much, much, longer though.

KITTIE: Oh please. I know how impatient you are.

VIOLA: You're the impatient one! I love the future you imagine, Kittie. It's heavenly. Race you to it?

KITTIE: You know I can never turn down a challenge.

(All the cyclists stop and create an isle for Kittie and Viola to race out of.)

VIOLA: Better hurry up, or I'll beat you!

(Viola rides off quickly.)

KITTIE: Wait, don't go! You know you can't beat me in a race, Viola!

(Kittie races off behind her, quickly gaining on her. The two women ride off into the distance laughing as William, Benzina, and Robert watch. Benzina steps forward.)

BENZINA: Those are my girls. Those are my girls, leaving me behind. Only five years after Viola's unexpected death, Kittie would pass away. On October 11th, 1900, Kittie Knox suddenly died from kidney disease. She was only 26, the same age Viola was when she died.

ROBERT TEAMOH: After all her exploits and mentions in the paper, her gravesite in Mount Auburn Cemetery was quickly forgotten as a spot of significance.

WILLIAM HAMILTON: But her story would be remembered again, after some decades and a new century.

ROBERT TEAMOH: You can see her mural at Cambridge Crossing.

WILLIAM HAMILTON: You can read her name on bike paths.

BENZINA: And hear it on Kittie Knox days proclaimed by the mayors of Cambridge and Boston.

ROBERT TEAMOH: The League even has an award named after her.

BENZINA: And you can know her story like we do. I'm tired of my girls leaving me here. I'm racing off to meet them. Enjoy fourth and fifth place, boys.

(Benzina quickly mounts her bike and rides off in the same direction of Kittie and Viola.)

ROBERT TEAMOH: Very unfair, Benzina! You didn't give us a proper warning!

(Robert mounts his bike and rides off.)

WILLIAM HAMILTON: Catch us if you can.

(William mounts his bike and starts riding. The cyclists ride off together into the distance.)

—— End of Play ——

Full Cast

THE HISTORY

Historical Character Biographies

Katherine "Kittie" Knox (1874–1900) was born in East Cambridge, Massachusetts, to John Knox, a Black tailor originally from Philadelphia, and Katherine Towle, a White seamstress originally from rural Maine. Kittie's father died, and she and her mother and older brother moved to the West End of Boston. Kittie became a seamstress and dress maker and an avid cyclist, joining the League of American Wheelmen (L.A.W.) around 1893. A vibrant personality, she was a frequent subject of the cycling press, as she pushed racial and gender barriers (she dared to wear bloomers). She was a popular figure at social events and dances and briefly became a cycling performer in minstrel shows in Boston and New York. Kittie died of kidney disease at age 26 at Massachusetts General Hospital. She is buried at Mount Auburn Cemetery.

Benzina (Reese) Gray (1873–1946): Originally from South Carolina, she moved to Cambridgeport with her uncle for opportunity and social freedom. She and Kittie cycled together on Martha's Vineyard. Her cousin, George Lewis, was secretary of the all-Black Riverside Cycling Club (R.C.C.). She initially worked as an office worker, and in 1902 she married Frederick Sanford Gray, a chef. She became a hotel cook in Plymouth and had three children.

Viola (Wheaton) Hamilton (1869–1895) was originally from Cleveland, Ohio, where she was known as a singer and pianist. She and three of her brothers moved to Massachusetts, and in September 1893 she married William Hamilton in Boston. She died of acute appendicitis in September 1895.

William Hamilton (1863–1939) was born in Boston's West End and grew up in Cambridgeport. He served as president of the R.C.C. from 1894–1895. Following the death of his first wife, he married Viola Wheaton in 1893. He was a singer in various choral groups and quartets, including the Riverside Male Quartette at Union Baptist Church on Main Street, Cambridge, next door to the R.C.C. clubhouse. He married his third wife, Mary, in 1897.

Robert Teamoh (1865–1912) was born in Boston and educated at the Boston Latin School. Another barrier-breaker, Robert was the first Black reporter for *The Boston Globe* and served as the West End's State Representative from 1894–1895. He wrote a bill designed to guarantee Black citizens the right to public accommodations and another against the L.A.W. color bar. In addition to being a racing judge for the R.C.C., he was a member of the Prince Hall Masons, president of the Crispus Attucks Club, and founding president of the short-lived "Greater Boston Baseball League." He married Julia Jackson in 1894, and they had one child, Robert Shaw Teamoh.

Charley Percival (1872–1940) was a journalist, cyclist, and entrepreneur. An active member of the Press Cycling Club, he served as editor of cycling magazines and was an L.A.W. official (including judging a cycling costume competition in Waltham in 1895, where he awarded Kittie first prize). While he served as head of the Massachusetts chapter of the Century Road Club of America, he explicitly advertised a ride without a color bar. His interests varied—he studied medicine and wrote for pseudo-medical journals, served in the First World War, and became involved in auto journalism, sales, and endurance racing. He had a tumultuous series of three marriages.

Colonel William Wagner Watts (1860–1924) was the leader of the Louisville, Kentucky chapter of the L.A.W.; he fought to pass a color bar into the L.A.W. constitution. An arch-segregationist, Watts was a lawyer and member of the Kentucky militia.

Abbot Bassett (1845–1924) was born in Chelsea, Massachusetts. Bassett was a journalist and newspaper publisher and then switched to bicycling publications. He was national Secretary of the L.A.W., but despite his deep influence, he was unsuccessful in preventing the color bar from being passed into the L.A.W. constitution.

Mary Sargent Hopkins (1846–1924) was born in Lynn, Massachusetts. She published *The Wheelwoman*, the only national cycling publication geared towards women. She believed that cycling promotes good health for women but also strongly opposed bloomers and fast riding. In the early 1900s, she moved to New York City.

John J. Walsh (1871–1949) was born in Dublin, Ireland; he emigrated to the United States when he was five years old. He graduated from Boston University Law School, practiced law, and became active in politics. He also served as President of the Malden Bicycle Club in 1896. He married Ethel Armitadge in 1893, but had the marriage annulled when he discovered that a career as a Catholic politician was incompatible with having a Protestant wife.

Ethel Armitage Walsh (1874–unknown) grew up in Rowley, Massachusetts. She married John J. Walsh in 1893. They had two children.

Fred St. Onge (1874–1939) was born in Cambridge, Massachusetts and became a racer, trick rider, riding instructor, and vaudevillian (United States, Asia, Australia, South Africa, and Europe). He sponsored cycling festivals and promoted bicycle safety for riders, especially children. He taught Helen Keller to ride tandem. During the early days of film, Fred relocated to Hollywood.

TIMELINE

1893—Kittie Knox joined the League of American Wheelmen at a time when few women were members.

1894—the League of American Wheelmen instituted a "color bar" by amending its constitution to restrict membership to "White" cyclists only. This policy formalized racial exclusion during the 1890s cycling boom, targeting Black cyclists like Marshall "Major" Taylor. The color bar was forgotten, and then formally repudiated, by the League's successor organization in 1999.

1896—Plessy v. Ferguson. Homer Plessy was a mixed-race man who boarded a Whites-only train to protest the Louisiana Separate Car Act. The ruling in this Supreme Court case upheld a Louisiana state law that allowed for equal but separate accommodations for the White and Colored races.

1920—The 19th Amendment to the Constitution gave women the right to vote.

1967—Loving v. Virginia. The U.S. Supreme Court unanimously struck down all remaining state laws banning marriage between individuals of different races.

Jennnifer Drummond, Dustin Teuber, Hampton Richards

HISTORICAL NOTES

by Lorenz J. Finison

Cycling

Modern cycling began in the early 1870s, and the Boston Bicycling Club, a gentlemen's organization, was founded in 1878. They raced and toured on high wheeled bicycles. Women and men who could not vault up into a high wheeler seat started riding large-wheeled tricycles. They formed clubs to take leisurely rides into the countryside. By the late 1880s, "safety" bicycles began to appear. They had equal-sized wheels, cushioned tires, and chains. Some had brakes. Women's bikes had a curved frame to fit a long dress, and chain guards to avoid the dress being caught in the chain. But this drop frame had to be heavier than a man's "diamond" frame to be strong enough. Kittie and other young fast-riding women chose the diamond frame.

The greater speed and lower price of safety bicycles attracted many different sorts of people to cycling. In the mid-1890s, cycling was more popular than baseball, football, and the new sport of basketball, but only men could race under League of American Wheelmen ("League") regulations. It was feared that women who rode fast would publicly sweat, develop a "bicycle face" from the strain and a "bicycle hump" from bending over the handlebars.

Many state militias in New England started Bicycle Units. The all-Black Company L of the 6th Regiment, Massachusetts Volunteer Militia, had its own Black officers and had an armory in the West End near Kittie's home. Many members were West End or Cambridge cyclists and members of the Riverside Cycle Club. They paraded on bicycles with other militia units and got special praise from the Governor of Massachusetts.

Southern bicycle clubs agitated to kick Black cyclists out of the League and succeeded in 1894. Massachusetts and several other states tried to resist the color bar but lost the final vote.

Cycling declined, and by the 1900s, it was almost gone. Bike clubs, cycling reporters, and news disappeared. Gentlemen cyclists joined the newly forming country clubs to get away from the sights and smells of the city, and its immigrants. They started riding and racing motorcycles, and eventually, automobiles. The automobile took advantage of the League's "Good Roads" campaign. Cycling rolled slowly on—the Bicycling Bust—until the 1970s, when the environmental movement aroused great interest in it again—a Bicycling Renaissance.

Race

Black Americans looked forward to a better life with freedom from slavery after the 13th Amendment to the Constitution was passed in 1865. The 14th Amendment (passed in 1868) guaranteed citizenship, and then the 15th Amendment (passed in 1870) got Black men the right to vote. A Public Accommodations law prohibiting discrimination passed in 1875, but a reaction came on in full force, amid the emergence of the Ku Klux Klan. Federal troops were withdrawn from the Confederate states in 1877, and there was no real obstacle the reassertion of White supremacy. The Public Accommodations law was overturned by the Supreme Court in 1883.

A massive growth in anti-Black (Jim Crow) laws and practices in the South affected northern culture and politics too, even in that hotbed of Abolitionism—Boston. In addition, laws like the Chinese Exclusion Act (1882) and the growth of the Immigration Restriction League (1894) created opposition to immigrants. A wave of demeaning cartoons, vaudeville acts, minstrel shows, parade floats, advertisements, and songs—cycling songs, too— mocked Black citizens and immigrants.

In Boston cycling clubs, too, there were steps backward to fall in line with the national movement against Black and immigrant rights. For example, Sterling Elliott, President of the League, who had been a supporter of Kittie Knox in 1895, changed his mind, and Kittie's White ally, Charles Percival, was slapped down by the national leadership of the Century Road Club of America for promoting a century ride with *no* color bar.

Kittie's time was a time of increasing challenges to Black rights. The fight for rights reached another peak in the 1950s and 1960s, but threats continue.

Gender

In Kittie's big year of 1895, the right of women to vote was still twenty-five years away. A national cultural conflict went on between "modern" women (the New Woman or Coming Woman) and their male allies, versus the traditionalists (many men but some women, too). They opposed women's suffrage (the vote), modern dress style—also known as "rational dress"—careers outside the home, freedom to travel, to own property (if married), in inheritance, and in many other ways.

Some cycling women banded together under the umbrella of *The Wheelwoman* and its publisher Mary Sargent Hopkins. The magazine boosted cycling but insisted that women should wear dresses and portray a lady-like image. Yet, they had to deal with the increasing adoption of bloomers by fast-riding, younger women like Kittie Knox.

The suffrage movement was divided over the question of race. The National American Women's Suffrage Association was not committed to Black social and political rights. As Kittie Knox moved to the West End, Josephine St. Pierre Ruffin started a new club and journal called *Women's Era.* They carried pro-Black suffragist messages. Ruffin was a speaker at anti-lynching protests held at the Charles Street AME Church, just a few blocks from Kittie's home, and in 1895 she organized the first National Conference of Colored Women in America in Boston. The Church also hosted protests of the League's color bar and many other barriers. So, Kittie Knox's neighborhood was a hotbed of political activism. While the newspapers never mention her speaking at the rallies, they likely influenced her determination to continue her pedaling ways, despite the barriers.

THE PRODUCTION

The Kittie Knox Plays 2025 World Premiere

September 13—Cambridge Crossing, Cambridge, MA

September 20—The Eustis Estate, Milton, MA

September 27—Herter Park, Boston, MA

Playwrights—Kirsten Greenidge, Patrick Gabridge, & Claire Soleil Gardner

Directed by Michelle Aguillon

Cast:

Kittie Knox . . . . Hampton Richards

Benzina Reese. . . . . Rebekah Brunson

Viola Hamilton (Wheaton) . . . . Beyoncé Martinez

William Hamilton . . . . .Nathan Johnson

Robert Teamoh. . . . . Joshua Lee Robinson

Mary Sargent Hopkins . . . . Jennifer Drummond

Abbot Bassett/Mr. Walsh .Tom Berry

Merrie Wheeler/Gertrude Parker/Mrs. Walsh . . . . Em Sheeran

Charley Percival/Col. Watts/Fred St. Onge . . . . Dustin Teuber

Musicians:

Elise Brown, Nick Chieffo, Lee Forrest

Understudies:

Kittie, Benzina, Viola . . . . Victoria Lee

Abbot, Walsh, Charley, Watts, Fred . . . . Thomas Vice

Mary, Merrie Wheeler, Gertrude, Mrs. Walsh. . . . Abby Kesselman

Robert, William . . . . .Trevor G. Frederick

Production Team:

Lead Producer . . . . Hannah McEachern

Stage Manager . . . . Katelyn Paddock

Assistant Stage Manager . . . . Jolie Frazer

Costume Designer . . . . Carol Benson Antos

Wardrobe Supervisor. . . . . Lonnie Miller

Music Director . . . . Nicholas Chieffo

Choreographer . . . . Hampton Richards

Props Designer. . . . . Lily McCollum

Plays in Place Fundraising Manager. . . . . Morgan Henderson

Box Office Manager / Plays in Place Co-Producer. . . . . . . Jess Meyer

Historical Consultant . . . . Lorenz J. Finison

Producing Artistic Director . . . . Patrick Gabridge

PLAYWRIGHT'S REFLECTION

by Claire Soleil Gardner (*To the Cliffs of Gay Head*)

To tell Kittie Knox's story was a huge responsibility. I was invited into the project by Patrick Gabridge, Artistic Director of Plays in Place, at an ice cream shop shortly after I graduated from Boston University's School of Theatre. When Pat told me Kittie's life story, I related to her as a young woman with big ambitions, just getting started in life. I was inspired by Kittie's fearlessness in the face of any physical, social, or political obstacle that stood between her and her passion for cycling. I was honored and excited to be writing alongside my former professor, Kirsten Greenidge, whose mentorship was pivotal in my development as a playwright. We were all joined by historian Larry J. Finison as we began our research.

At the beginning of the process, it was undecided what events in Kittie's life each of us would adapt into plays. We learned about her childhood in the West End and her career as a talented seamstress, whose earnings allowed her to own a bicycle and join the Boston-based cycling craze. While cycling clubs offered an active social scene, they were accompanied by the racial prejudices inherent in the increasingly segregated society of the 1890s. We discussed whether to call Kittie an activist, because it was difficult to ascertain how she viewed herself, as there are no diaries or writings from her. Nonetheless, her physical feats and brave actions to demand her inclusion were widely reported in the popular press and cycling journals. Sources such as newspaper columns often used outdated, offensive language to refer to her bi-racial identity, which made the bias of our sources clear and obscured the truth. I was especially drawn to reports of Kittie's insistence on attending and dancing at the balls held at cycling meets. Her gowns, which were undoubtedly self-made or altered, were always reported upon and images of them captured my imagination.

Hampton Richards

I was determined to write about Kittie attending one of these balls, in a gorgeous gown, surrounded by cyclists and perhaps even dancing on a bicycle. While writing the first drafts of our plays, we were unsure how the bicycles would fit in. The precedent for bicycles in plays was either stationary bikes or bikes ridden merely for entrances and exits. I wanted the cycling to be entwined into the action of my play, and the term 'bikeography' became my method. Thanks to the creative staging of our director, Michelle Aguillon, the 'bikeography' of my imagination came to life. Writing the ball was an incredible challenge and to succeed, it meant my play would be the final play in our trilogy. This added the challenge of also having to summarize the first two plays and tie all three together in a coherent conclusion. Inspired by Kittie's example and her indefatigable spirit, I couldn't turn away. To be a part of this project, sharing Kittie's story and memory, has been a great honor.

DIRECTOR'S REFLECTION

by Michelle Aguillon

When I first started working on *The Kittie Knox Plays*, the big question on everyone's minds was how to stage these plays on bikes... and outdoors. The prospect never scared me. In fact, it intrigued me. I looked forward to breaking staging conventions, being outdoors, and riding bikes.

Thank goodness we workshopped the plays numerous times as this helped a great deal with planning. It was a blessing to be able to work with the playwrights who made themselves available for rewrites and edits from the first readings and all the way through final rehearsals. And it was thrilling to be able to rely on our Boston-based pool of actors. There were many actors who worked with us at one time or another in the process of developing these new scripts. With every iteration, I was fine-tuning the staging, thinking about the costuming needs (long skirts on bikes were essential since Kittie lived in the late-nineteenth century), safety (of course), learning how to deal with the outdoor public spaces, and figuring out how to support the vocal prowess and physical stamina the actors needed, especially in the summer heat.

We tested out the plays on bikes for the first time during a warm, fall weekend at Cambridge Crossing. It was exciting to see the actors on bikes. We discovered the comedy, realized staging challenges, and discovered what was going to be our biggest challenge: volume. We knew going into those big expansive spaces that volume would be a huge challenge, but we really didn't know to what extent until that weekend.

When we officially started rehearsals a year later, we rehearsed in the three different outdoor spaces, each with their own set of specific challenges. Cars, trains, helicopters, pedestrian traffic, and large glass buildings bouncing voices was what we had to work with at Cambridge Crossing. Our time at Herter Park brought us BBQ parties, drum and dance classes, and live sports events at nearby Harvard Stadium. My favorite space was the very quiet, remote Eustis Estate in Milford outside of Boston; it was an expansive property with an old, renovated mansion. Surrounding it were paths bordered with trees, but also neighbors with active driveways. Airplanes doing their final approach overhead to Logan Airport were also a big noise challenge there. We learned why the Ancient Greeks performed facing forward almost the entirety of performance. It was the only way to hear all the words! Turning ever so slightly profile to say dialogue to fellow actors was death to volume.

The plays were extremely physical, and each actor worked hard and generously, pivoting quickly when needed. They were inventive and malleable with every new idea to better support the play and each other, which ultimately shone through in the performances. Working on *The Kitty Knox Plays* and with this cast and production team was a great joy for me. I couldn't be prouder to have worked on such a unique show.

Michelle Aguillon, Director

ACTORS' REFLECTIONS

Hampton Richards (Kittie Knox)

Every time we rehearsed or performed on our bikes, I always had the thought that Kittie would be so proud. Proud that I can bike freely in the city of Cambridge and Boston. She fought courageously for the right for everyone to enjoy the freedom that was bike riding. This show made me fall in love with biking again. The words of the play rang true as I spoke them because I loved feeling the wind in my face and racing against my friends to see who was the fastest. I made sure I did not take her work for granted.

This show also gave me the chance to connect with fellow Black women on and off stage. The friendship was always genuine and fun onstage and so our relationships deepened offstage. I feel like we all held onto each other during this process and took care of each other. My fondest memories of the show are definitely with these women, and I felt like Kittie was similar in prioritizing her friendships.

Rebekah Brunson (Benzina Reese)

Working on *The Kittie Knox Plays* was such a fulfilling and beautiful experience. Having been a part of the process since it was in its reading stages, seeing it come to fullness was an indescribable feeling. I was honored to play Benzina Reese, a Massachusetts transplant by way of South Carolina. Coming from the Carolinas myself, it meant so much to me to infuse parts of my identity and my experience of domestic culture shock into the character. I rarely get to see Black Southerners on stage in a piece of work that isn't solely about trauma, enslavement, or injustice. I think Pat, Kirsten, and Claire, our playwrights, did an exceptional job of ensuring that the audience understood the injustices that Benzina faced, but also recognized the fullness of her personhood.

Collaborating with this team was an absolute dream. I look back on this process with so much happiness and gratitude. It was no small feat to memorize the blocking and cycling paths (in SKIRTS, no less!) for three different locations, but I felt so encouraged by Michelle, our director, that everything I needed was within me. Though the rehearsal process was brief, Michelle ensured that we had ample time to discuss our characters' motivations, personalities, and histories. I felt that I was deeply connected to Benzina Reese as well as Kittie Knox and Viola (Wheaton) Hamilton by the end of this process.

The bonds of sisterhood are immense and unbreakable for the Black women represented in this show. Playing and imagining the lives of Benzina, Kittie, and Viola alongside Hampton Richards, Beyoncé Martinez, and Victoria Lee is an experience that I will treasure forever. History and the theatre are two of my greatest loves, and I'm overjoyed to have seen them married through working on this production. I'm so proud to have performed in plays that bring light to a trailblazer—Kittie Knox—who history should never again forget.

Beyoncé Martinez (Viola Hamilton)

As a woman of color, having the opportunity to tell the story of an extraordinary Black woman like Kittie Knox is truly an opportunity of a lifetime. As a fellow history lover, being part of

Beyoncé Martinez, Rebekah Brunson, Hampton Richards

a production as meaningful as *The Kittie Knox Plays* is an experience I will never forget. It is essential that stories like Kittie's are told with care and by the right people, and Plays in Place could not have done a better job creating that space. The cast and crew were some of the most creative, funny, and down-to-earth people I have ever met. As someone who is just beginning to work professionally, I learned so much simply by watching them work and I felt incredibly privileged to be surrounded by dedicated, talented, and kind individuals. During moments of doubt, they lifted me up without even realizing it.

My favorite part of the experience was, of course, acting on bikes. Never did I imagine I would be part of a show that combined period costumes, biking, and outdoor performance during a Boston summer. Each day brought new challenges—whether it was my skirt getting caught in my bike gears onstage or the noise of the city competing with our voices—but we faced those challenges together as an ensemble. That sense of teamwork made every day feel lighter and reminded me why giving my all was always worth it.

Nathan Johnson (William Hamilton)

I spend a lot of time thinking and placing myself into the shoes of others. Mostly because I find the human experience fascinating in a plethora of aspects . . . but honestly, I find I learn plenty on the person I'm living through, and in equal parts I learn plenty about myself in what comes through telling the story of someone so different, or someone from a different world altogether.

Acting in *The Kittie Knox Plays* allowed me to experience a fear I hold within myself, but do not express for fear of spiraling into a nihilistic abyss consisting of a terrorizing, unrelenting, cascading wave of dire dread and unresolved angst. James Baldwin is quoted as saying, "To be a Negro in this country and to be relatively conscious is to be in a state of rage almost, almost all of the time—and in one's work."

As a Black man portraying a man in this story already rifled with that same rage and a healthy dose of fear in William Hamilton, I often found myself within this story exploring levels of sadness, fear, and apprehension that Patrick was able to express so flawlessly with the dialogue. I am grateful to not only have had the opportunity to speak these words, but to also safely explore this avenue of Black American history.

William Hamilton is a man who, by the end of the story, has lost two wives by means he had no control over. William lives in a world that ultimately is not in his control.

Performing this story by way of a bicycle was brilliant in the sense that this was one area that allowed not only control by way of the rider, but also once again as a Black man having any area of control was significant. The world opens to you on a bicycle. Suddenly, where you can be is only a matter of pedaling, weaving, steering, and rushing to your destination . . . I say all this to say that this was an important story to be told. I found myself taking in the true weight of the story as I rode on the roads several other Black riders rode on, and I found myself weeping at times when realizing my place in all of this, and on the same ride smiling the same way I hope they did as the world opened up to them, riding along the horizon into the light of day.

Nathan Johnson

Tom Berry (Abbot Bassett/Mr. Walsh)

As a young boy, I spent a lot of hours on my trusty red Schwinn bike. The wind in my face and the fresh air in my lungs propelled me and never failed to lift my spirits. I never dreamed that someday I would be spending my summer rehearsing in beautifully scenic locations, culminating in three glorious, sunny September Saturday performances of *The Kittie Knox Plays.*

In my years as an actor, I've performed on boats in Boston Harbor, in public parks, comedy clubs, restaurants, and even while being followed throughout the Boston Public Library. These experiences were steppingstones that prepared me for this project and the distinct settings we navigated to create three unique worlds with the same set of plays. Each site brought a sense of discovery and freshness to the plays.

It was an honor and an absolute joy to be a part of the development of this project, and to learn more about Ms. Knox, the history of cycling, and the influencers of the sport through the characters I embodied. Kittie herself rose above the challenges of her time with her own sense of joy for cycling that propelled her forward. The reaction I heard from audiences proved that message resonated. Our production was imbued from top to bottom with an infectious spirit of camaraderie and heart. I am thankful for the playwrights, production staff, crew, and fellow castmates with whom I was fortunate enough to embrace this project. It reinvigorated my love for theater and bicycling, and I am forever grateful to have been a part of this team.

Vicki Lee (understudy)

I was hesitant at first to take on the role of an understudy, not only because I would have to learn three different tracks of three very different women but also because before this production, I did not have the faintest clue how to ride a bike. This production forced me to acquire a new lifelong skill, which was mentally and physically demanding because we had to juggle the physicality of the bikes, embody our characters, memorize numerous blocking patterns, all while in period attire. And I would not trade this experience for the world; I had the best time. Being a part of *The Kittie Knox Plays* meant I could learn something new about myself and the characters I portrayed every day. I learned how tenacity drove Kittie forward to do incredible things, how Viola's quick wit never failed to surprise me and make me laugh and how Benzina's soft spoken manner would sometimes break when she had to mediate between both Kittie and Viola. And how sisterhood bound them all together.

Sisterhood was not whisked out of thin air but was already prevalent the first day of rehearsal along with my fellow actors. We bonded on serious topics, such as being Black women in the theatre industry and more trivial topics like *Love Island*. There was an immediate understanding and respect for who we were as actors and more importantly, as people. I will always fondly remember the summer of 2025 as "The Summer Girls Era."

PRODUCER'S REFLECTION

by Hannah McEachern

My work on the production began in January 2025, when I hopped on board the Plays in Place team—bright-eyed, bushy-tailed, and tasked with this behemoth of a project: nine actors, nine bikes, three different venues, and, ultimately, nine different blocking patterns. As a producer, that's a lot to keep track of, and the only reason this show was as successful as it was, was the extraordinary team we assembled.

Most of my work leading up to rehearsals involved hiring creative team members, running auditions, casting actors, connecting with venue owners, conducting site visits, and sending emails—*so many* emails. By the time rehearsals began in August, we were reveling in the warmth of the sun and each other's company. Everyone in the cast and creative team fully bought into our shared vision of bringing this trilogy of plays to life. And why wouldn't they? It's an incredible story of a strong, unapologetic woman fighting for, and earning, her place in a world that wasn't made for her.

Each of the three plays offers a different glimpse into Kittie's life: her girlish charm, her brutish speed, her wicked tongue. She is utterly captivating, and it amazed me that it took this long to learn about her. With the help of our Historical Consultant, Larry J. Finison, we were able to capture her spirit in a 90-minute outdoor experience that I believe would have thrilled Kittie herself.

Whether you're a teacher seeking a new play for your students, a bicycle club interested in sharing Kittie's story, or an ambitious theatre company exploring innovative modes of storytelling, *The Kittie Knox Plays* have much to offer. The plays provide rich, relatable roles for actors while illuminating a pivotal moment in history at the intersection of gender, race, fashion, transportation, and community. Kittie constantly defied societal expectations. From her ideas about marriage, to the clothes she wore, or the bike she rode, to the events she attended, she risked her life daily simply by having the audacity to want more for herself.

Kittie's story reminds us that the struggles of the 1890s are not so far removed from the realities of today. Women and people of color continue to be disrespected, overlooked, excluded, and harmed in an increasing number of ways. Her life is a powerful reminder that the fight is not over, and that the road toward true equality, peace, and justice is still long.

Producing these plays requires a team that shares the vision, understands the importance of the story, and is ready to do whatever it takes to make it happen. Fortunately, that's exactly what we had, and it's why all nine of our performances sold out or exceeded capacity. To tell Kittie's story, you must embody her audacity, grit, and determination, and with the right people, it won't feel like work at all. It'll feel like an honor.

Hannah McEachern, Producer

STAGE MANAGER'S REFLECTION

by Katelyn Paddock

Stage managing *The Kittie Knox Plays* was one of the most unique theatrical experiences I have been a part of. The interaction with the public and natural world, coupled with a cast of nine on bikes, was such a fun puzzle to figure out. For future stage managers, I recommend creating paperwork and systems for managing the bikes early in the process. My ASM Jolie and I created a spreadsheet detailing which bike belonged to which actor, with a list of swaps that would need to happen if understudies went on. We also had a running maintenance log where we tracked problems with the bikes and who was assigned to fixing them.

Safety was our top priority; we made sure at the top of each rehearsal, every bike was "safety checked" by a member of the SM team. Additionally, we taught the actors how to perform a safety check of their own and scheduled 5 minutes at the top of each rehearsal or performance for them to take a lap on their bikes and tell us if they noticed a problem. If they encountered any issues mid-show, we collaborated with the director to come up with various contingency plans to get them to the end of the scene, at which point their bike could be taken offstage to get checked or swapped out.

Since we were performing in large outdoor spaces, many of our presets, entrances, and exits were set up several yards from the "playing space." This meant that when an actor started to bike in, it could be anywhere from fifteen seconds to one minute before they made it to center stage. Our stage crew used walkie talkies to communicate with each other. I stood slightly behind the audience where I could see every point of approach and called standbys and gos to the crew at the entrance and exit points; the crew would translate this to the actors through visual gestures. Early in the process, we timed out about how long it would take to bike from an entrance point to center stage—this was hugely helpful when we got to tech and needed to figure out the placement of these cues.

Katelyn Paddock, Stage Manager

On a personal note, *The Kittie Knox Plays* reaffirmed that a sense of spontaneity and flexibility is one of the most important things a stage manager can embody. When faced with confused members of the public, parking issues, and more, we quickly assessed, made a plan, and said, "let's try it!" As I continue onto new projects, I will be taking that "let's try it" spirit with me, and I encourage future stage managers of *The Kittie Knox Plays* to do so, too.

COSTUME DESIGNER'S REFLECTION

by Carol Benson Antos

The story of Kittie Knox appealed to me on so many levels that I was eager to be part of this production and bring Kittie and her contemporaries to life for a modern audience. She was a trailblazing biracial woman, a competitive cyclist, a talented seamstress, and was willing to embrace the highly controversial fashion of wearing bloomers/knickers, even if it meant her ankles would be seen by men. Oh, horrors! (Societal control of female attire resonated personally, having grown up in an era when the length of our skirts was arbitrarily determined and girls were not allowed to wear pants to school.)

For me, costume design begins with learning about the characters, in this case real people. Fortunately, historical records are available for some of the individuals in *The Kittie Knox Plays* providing information on age, race, occupation, social status, interests, and location. From the scripts, I learned what was happening in their lives, how they viewed the world and clues to their personalities. Documentation from the League of American Wheelmen, *The Wheelwoman*, and historical photographs provided information—but also challenges.

For example, there are accounts of what Kittie was wearing when she won the prize for best costume which dictated the color and fabric to use in our production, but we worried whether wool would be too warm in late summer in Boston. And since the plays would be performed outdoors, the overriding (no pun intended) concern about catching long skirts in the gear mechanism of modern bicycles meant hours of practice and a few greasy rips that needed attention.

Where, when and how Kittie (and the rest of the cast) would be able to change costumes as scenes moved from recreational cycling on Martha's Vineyard and Medford, to the annual meet in Asbury Park, to an elegant ball in Boston also required some brainstorming. Some changes needed to occur on stage, requiring assistance from other actors built into the blocking and dialogue.

Nathan Johnson, Joshua Lee Robinson, Hampton Richards, Beyoncé Martinez, Rebekah Brunson

Fortunately, the cast and crew from Plays in Place worked together to overcome these challenges. It's that creative process and willingness to be flexible and resourceful that defines the theatrical experience for me and keeps generations of us inspired to join together to keep telling these important stories.

MUSIC DIRECTOR'S REFLECTION

by Nicholas Chieffo

Developing a new play is always endlessly thrilling. When there are three of them, in succession, with sound and music, performed outside, the layers compound and evolve. The content could exceed in any context; this ambitious arrangement was a success through compassionate organization, diligent attention to detail, and conscious investment in experimentation. These elements were abundant across every member of this large team.

We had time to experiment with this piece. This is vital to any piece of work, and it was certainly no different here. We had access to different outdoor locations on some sunny, and brisk, fall days. These vignettes were already teeming with life, zeal, and fervor.

The roles of the sound and music did not differ much from any other project, in my eyes (and ears). It is there to develop and highlight the emotional texture of the piece. We approached the project like any other, with its own novel challenges, solutions, and goals. I continue to find it valuable to involve myself early in the process. I find just observing in the rehearsal room to be helpful. I listen to the rhythms in the lines, the melody in the actors, the beats. What does the production want to emphasize? In conjunction, Director Michelle Aguillon and I met to discuss what moments, what feelings we want to support.

In the arrangements, we attempted to capture some sound of that era, and of (as Larry J. Finison states), the Cycling Craze. Of those sounds, we utilized songs in the public domain. Songs became thematic for people and ideas. *The Scorcher* played while we saw Kittie and her friends. We played a haughty, militaristic *Daisy Bell* to reflect Mary Sargent Hopkins' rigid and backwards ideology. Sound helped transition the location, guiding us through a travel montage from Boston to New York to New Jersey.

Of course, these ideas were supported and developed by the indispensable knowledge and creative work of musicians, Lee Forrest and Elise Brown. There was tenacity and patience as I arranged the pieces, then rearranged them to adjust for volume, or to sound richer, or to sound less rich, all while balancing as we sat on sloped hills, or in three different spots for each play.

In the logistical context of the band, our whole system needed to be mobile. We distilled our abundant instruments, stands, and chairs, to fit snugly in a rolling cart. We found that wind blew the stands over or blew the music right off the stand. We built sandbags out of canvas pencil cases to weigh down the stands. Sheets were attached not with flimsy clothespins, but with small magnets. Copies of cue sheets and music were preset in every area.

A pitfall that I believe we not only avoided, but conquered, is the stuffy, reserved rhythm that seems to plague historical plays. This was anything but that, instead dynamic and dancey, top to bottom.

Art in public spaces is necessary. Its challenges, like people walking by, gawking and intrigued, are part of the charm. I have the feeling Kittie would have enjoyed the public captivation. The unwavering dynamic nature of the piece is essential—it reflects just some of the enterprising spirit that Kittie embodied. It is a unique play because she and her friends were unique people. I hope that we were able to honor some of that. The bicycling beacon she built is intrinsic to the fabric of Boston's DNA, and to the call for liberation and freedom for all.

Lee Forrest, Elise Brown, Nicholas Chieffo, The God d*mn Brass Band

TIPS & TRICKS FOR A SUCCESSFUL PRODUCTION

by Lead Producer, Hannah McEachern, and
Producing Artistic Director, Patrick Gabridge

Our company has extensive experience creating new site-specific productions at a wide variety of sites. We've created plays at historic cemeteries, 300-year-old churches, barns, and even in the Senate Chamber of the Massachusetts State House. Every project and site is a challenging new puzzle. This project was actually more "bike-specific" than "site-specific"—the use of bikes was even more critical than the locations.

Our 2025 production of *The Kittie Knox Plays* featured nine actors, nine bikes, three musicians, and four understudies. We performed the plays in three very different park-like settings on three consecutive Saturdays, performing the set of plays three times on each of those days (11 a.m., 2 p.m., 4:30 p.m.). Each play was in a slightly different location, with seating in 60 folding chairs. Audiences moved between performance spots on foot, following a staff member and the musicians. Actors always moved in and out of scenes while riding their bikes, and they also moved between plays by bike.

All sounds/music were created live by the three-person band that was part of the show. We did not build any additional sets or add any lighting and did not use sound amplification or mics. Costume changes were generally made in a pop-up tent with walls, set slightly out of view.

Tickets were free but reservations were required. Houses were always full and we attracted much interest from passersby.

If you're considering producing these plays, whether outdoors or indoors, we want to share some things we've learned from our production:

- How you choose to incorporate bikes is up to your discretion. Since our show was outdoors, our actors rode in and out of scenes on their bikes. However, if you're doing this indoors, or don't have good access to bikes, your creativity will be your superpower.

- If you choose to incorporate bikes, having someone onsite who is handy and has tools is a must. It may go without saying, but a bike pump is an essential tool for this show!

- When casting your actors, ask for their inseam, it's the best way to know what size bike they need.

- Make sure to build in some extra rehearsal time for getting the actors comfortable on bikes. Skirts can be a big challenge and require extra practice and care while riding.

- Bike storage can be a challenge. Our entire show fit in the back of a Ford Transit 250 cargo van. We needed to be completely mobile, because we were performing at a different site every weekend. Our team packed nine bikes, multiple props, costume boxes, and racks into that van every night like Tetris. God bless stage managers.

- However, if you live in a town with a bike share, you might be able to partner with them and use their bikes (and not need storage at all). BlueBikes in Boston let us use their bikes for free for our first outdoor play development day with bikes.

- Be in good communication with your venue contacts. Scheduling site-visits and establishing your day-of contacts for rehearsals and performances in advance is a must, especially if you're performing in a space that is heavily used by the public. Expect surprises—for one show, we learned at the last minute about a road race that started at our exact spot and made parking a nightmare. We adjusted, thanks to a brilliant box office manager, but it wasn't easy.

- In outdoor settings, we highly recommend signs pointing your audience to the box office check-in, and around the venue as they move from play to play if they're in different spots; it's important to consider the blissfully unaware stragglers.

- Our cast had varying levels of green room accommodations during performances. We booked a private dining room in a nearby restaurant for our first weekend, the historical site we performed at had a fully working apartment for the second weekend, and on our third weekend, we had a large tent in the park where we performed. Whatever your budget, just make sure your actors have access to bathrooms, adequate changing areas, and a pizza party between shows never hurts either.

- If you intend to produce these shows outdoors, your most common problem is likely to be noise, whether it's from buses, trains, nearby fitness-in-the-park, or airplanes overhead. Try to scout your site well in advance, and at the time of day when you plan to perform. Be sure to check the public events calendar if you're using parks or other programmed space.

- Our show performed three Saturdays in a row, for three 90-minute performances a day. If we did it again, we'd recommend doing only two shows per day—especially when it's late summer, it can get hot, and our cast experienced some fatigue by the last weekend with the long days we had.

- If you're producing outdoors, try to find cover or a backup space in case of rain. It will ease your stress to know you have options. We scheduled rain dates (Sundays) and held an indoor venue as a backup. (Thankfully, each Saturday of our run was beautiful, but we watched the forecast nervously every day.)

- If the show must go on, consider hiring understudies. We cast four understudies for this production: one Black man to cover William, and Robert, one Black woman to cover Kittie, Benzina, and Viola, one White man to cover Charlie/Fred/ Watts, and Abbott Bassett/John Walsh, and one White woman to cover Mary and Merrie/Gertrude/Ethel. We also contracted these actors as production assistants, so we automatically had four extra sets of hands for our production team. This show is an all-hands-on-deck situation, and our PAs were incredibly valuable.

- Get the community involved! Reach out to local biking organizations, nonprofit groups that support youth of color, or your local government to support the production of these plays. Having community support goes a long way.

- Find the FUN! As long as you assemble an amazing team you trust, you'll have an incredible amount of fun while juggling the pieces of this production. This play is very much about Bike Joy and Black Joy. Adding bikes makes every rehearsal and performance a lot more fun.

Beyoncé Martinez

FURTHER STUDY

Discussion Prompts

"The bicycle is the great emancipator." What freedoms did cycling enable, particularly for women and Black people, in the United States in the late-nineteenth century?

"I cannot overstate the importance, for women cyclists, to promote the proper decorum. In dress. In behavior." In the plays we see that Kittie Knox is wearing bloomers rather than a skirt. This divergence from societal expectations of how women dressed was seen as disrespectful and inappropriate by some in the establishment. Where else did you see social etiquette challenged in the plays and to what effect?

"Shout about all you've accomplished all over the place, 'til you're hoarse in the throat and blue in the face." What did you learn about Kittie Knox's accomplishments? How were they celebrated, and conversely, how were they dismissed or undermined?

Claire Soleil Gardner's play coins the word "bikeography" for choreography with bikes. How does cycling and the presence of bikes influence the way the plays tell their story? How would the plays be different if they were performed indoors and/or without bicycles?

From seagulls to formal music at a ball, what sounds did you notice in the play scripts? How does this soundscape mirror the sounds of the outdoors where the plays are performed today? What effect does this collision of past and present have?

Throughout the plays, the characters hear of political debates at the state and national levels that would affect their lives (such as the 1896 Supreme Court decision in Plessy v. Ferguson ruling that racial segregation laws did not violate the U.S. Constitution as long as the facilities for each race were equal in quality, a doctrine that came to be known as "separate but equal.") How do Kittie and her friends respond to hearing about these societal shifts? How does this mirror how regular people now talk about national political debates?

"What will my story be, if all that's left is what was said and printed behind my back?" How does the politics and opinion of the reporter (Mary Sargent Hopkins) effect cultural norms and the way Kittie is treated amongst her fellow cyclists? How do the more recent celebrations of her accomplishments such as naming a bike path after her and the creation of these plays serve as a living memorial? What affect does uncovering this erased history have for us now?

"I'm about to go to a ball with White people. Or did they only invite the White part of me, and expect the rest to be left at the door?" As a mixed-race woman, where does colorism enter Kittie's story? How does Kittie act differently when she is with her friends versus when she is in White society and amongst people who disapprove of her?

Did you hear anything in the play that you are curious to learn more about? What questions are you left with about the people, events, and times of the plays?

Beyoncé Martinez, Hampton Richards, Rebekah Brunson

BIBLIOGRAPHY

(For more information about the life and times of Kittie Knox.)

Finison, Lorenz J. *Boston's Cycling Craze, 1880–1890*. University of Massachusetts Press, 2014.

Finison, Lorenz J. *Boston's Twentieth Century Bicycling Renaissance: Cultural Change on Two Wheels*. Bright Leaf Publishers, 2019.

Finison, Lorenz J. "Kittie Knox, Boston Cyclist in the 1890s: The War Between Exclusion and Inclusion," in Robert Cyornak and Douglas Stark (Eds.), *Boston's Black Athletes: Identity, Performance, and Activism*. Lanham, MD: Lexington Books, 2024.

Goldberg, David E. *The Retreats of Reconstruction*. Fordham University Press, 2016.

Greenidge, Kerri. *Black Radical: The Life and Times of William Monroe Trotter*. Liveright, 2019.

Grover, Kathryn. *To Heal the Wounded Nation*. National Park Service, 2021.

Schneider, Mark Robert. *Boston Confronts Jim Crow, 1890–1920*. Northeastern University Press, 1997.

Wolff, Daniel. *Fourth of July, Asbury Park: A History of the Promised Land*. Bloomsbury, 2005.

Zheutlin, Peter. *Around the World on Two Wheels: Annie Londonderry's Extraordinary Ride*. Citadel Press, 2007.

Kittie Knox Legacy Archives
Materials about Kittie Knox's legacy, including *The Kittie Knox Plays*, are part of the Bicycling History Collections in University Archives and Special Collections at the University of Massachusetts, Boston. For more information visit archives.umb.edu and search "Kittie Knox" and then contact library. archives@umb.edu for access.

FUNDERS & SPECIAL THANKS

Donors who supported this publication:

Leslie Bennett

Virginia Brady

Jamie Carty

Darin Cook & Kristina Ramer

Larry Finison

Grace Hall

Pamela & Don Michaelis

Nan Millett

Jill Morawski

Lee Pelton

Wendy Schwartz

Mary Smoyer

Leon Wilson

Timothy Wilson

Christopher Yens & Temple Gill

Cynthia Zabin

Joshua Lee Robinson, Dustin Teuber, Rebekah Brunson

Donors who supported the development of the plays and the 2025 production:

Corporate Sponsors:

The Boston Foundation (Lee Pelton)

The Lawrence & Lillian Solomon Foundation

James M & Cathleen D. Stone Foundation

Cambridge Arts Council

Cambridge Community Foundation

DivcoWest

Historic New England

Individual Donors:

Betel Arnold

Paul Basken

Ezekiel Baskin

Catherine Bird

Robert Boulrice

Ginny Brady

Jan Brown

Lori Burlingham

Mary J. Carbonara

Frank Carbone

Jessica Chace

Thom Clelan

Ram Chavali

Darin Cook & Kristina Ramer

Ann Croston

Karen Delorey

Karen DeSimone

Stacey Dogan

Rose A. Doherty

Sally Ebeling

Julie Ecker

Harley Erdman

Ryan Evans & Darcy Duke

Carrie Finison

Lorenz J. Finison

Karl Finison

Sara Finison

Maria Foster

Bettye & Robert Freeman

Sheree Galpert

Lauren Gibbs

Patricia Grandieri

Sarah Grant

Grace Hall

Ralph & Janice Halpern

Jonina Herter

Carole Hirsch

Frank Jennings

Paul Kastner

Kathryn Keeler

John Kinsman

Matthew Knowlton

George Kohout

Shawn LaCount

Jamie Lin

Anne Marie Lindquist

Kimberly Lucas

Jeni Mahoney

Eric Mankin & Carol Yun

Christine Mastal

Catherine Matthews

Lincoln Mckie

Pamela & Don Michaelis

David Miller

Steven Miller

Nancy Towle Millett

Jeffrey Millett

Lydia Moland

Jeanne & Joel Mooney

Jean Monroe

Patricia & Raymond Monroe

Karl Moore

Bill Nesper, League of
American Bicyclists

Sarah Newhouse

Lynne O'Connell &
R. Lynn Rardin

Heather Pence

Eric Peterson

Diane Pierce-Williams

Alicia Powell

John Quatrale

Regina Rheault

Laura Roberts

Ilyse Robbins

Kathleen Rogers & Rick Teller

Karla Rosenstein

Melissa Rubinsky

Ann Schlesinger

Dan & Jill Schreiber

Wendy Schwartz

Kim Slack

Mary Smoyer

Patrice Snellings

Richard Snow

Jeffrey Song

Bob Stachel

Tim Swartz

Julia Trueblood

Eric Vanderpoel

David Veloz

D. Walters

Ann West

Williams Giving Fund

Wheel Wranglers

Kim Wolfson

Kaitlin Woods

Don & Agnes Woodlock

Xiaofeng Xia

Patricia Yingling

Jaclyn Youngblood

Special Thanks for the book and 2025 production:

Ben Rose, Production Photographer

Cambridge Crossing

Concord Players

DivcoWest

Emerson College

Friends of Herter Park

Historic New England & the Eustis Estate Staff

Jazzmin Bonner

Jes Slavin

Joe Juknievich

Jules Talbot

Katherine Shaver

Lyric Stage Company of Boston

MassBike, especially Galen Mook, Jes Slavin, & Emma Walter

Sami Ahmad, Production Videographer

Sean Condon, Speed & Sprocket Mobile Bike Shop

Stoller Sportswear

Teddy Harrington

Tracy Gabridge

Elizabeth Silver, Richie Wills, Kiran Asher, Helen Brown, Sarah Buttenwieser, and Stan the Fixit Man all loaned us bikes to use in the show.

Hampton Richards, Dustin Teuber

PLAYWRIGHTS

Patrick Gabridge

Patrick is the producing artistic director and founder of Plays in Place and has created site-specific plays in partnership with many museums and historic sites, including Mount Auburn Cemetery, Boston's Old State House, Old South Meeting House, Historic Northampton, and Old North Church, among others. He is an award-winning playwright and has written 24 historical plays, along with many contemporary plays that have received more than 1,000 productions from theatres and schools around the world (17 countries so far). He's also a screenwriter, novelist, and a writer of audio plays. Patrick, a longtime cyclist, published the blog Choosing No Car about his family's adventures with car-free life in Boston.

Claire Soleil Gardner

Claire (she/they) is a multi-disciplinary playwright, poet, director, dramaturg, and performer with a BFA in Theatre Arts from Boston University. A 2026 MacDowell Fellow for playwriting, Claire's play *DEVIL GIRL* was selected for LimeFest at The Tank, their play *Virtual Rez-ality* was selected for Native Voices Short Play Festival 2025, and they were a commissioned playwright with What Will the Neighbors Say? Claire performed the role of Zanj in *Into Your Hands* by Tomi Endter at The Public, performed the role of Moon in *Two Spirit F(l)ag* by Ty Defoe in the Say Gay Plays Festival, and was Assistant Director for *Number Our Days: A Photographic Oratorio* at the Perelman Performing Arts Center. Claire is a proud diasporic Métis-Cree individual whose passion for history, education, and social justice is central to their work.

Kirsten Greenidge

Village Voice/Obie and PEN America/Laura Pels winner, Kirsten is the author of *The Luck of the Irish, Milk Like Sugar, Our Daughters Like Pillars,* and *Common Ground: Revisited,* an adaptation of J. Anthony Lucas' Pulitzer Prize-winning book about Boston's desegregation efforts in the 1970s. A hallmark of Kirsten's work is her focus on the nexus of race, class, and gender in the United

States in the past and present. Her recent work includes *Matilde: A Fable*, commissioned by Oregon Shakespeare Festival and produced at the 2024 DNA Festival at La Jolla Playhouse, the libretto for *The Anonymous Lover*, an adaptation of the original by Joseph Bologne, which premiered at Boston Lyric Opera in 2024 and was presented at Opera Philly in 2025. Kirsten is an Associate Professor of Theatre at the School of Theatre at Boston University, where she oversees the playwrighting track of study and also serves as the school's director. Kirsten attended Wesleyan University and the Playwright's Workshop at the University of Iowa. She is currently working on commissions from A.R.T., Fourth Wall Theatricals, for which she is developing the musical *Shelter*, based on the journalism of Lauren Sandler, with music and lyrics by Crystal Monee Hall, which was workshopped at New York Stage and Film in 2025. Her work on an adapted libretto of Gaetano Donizetti's *Daughter of the Regiment* was presented in April 2026.

Patrick Gabridge, Kirsten Greenidge, Claire Soleil Gardner

Plays in Place was founded in 2018 and since then has collaborated with countless cultural institutions to develop and produce new site-specific plays. We've created theatre for historic churches, iconic cemeteries, New England Meeting Houses, and even the Senate Chamber of the Massachusetts State House. Our plays engage audiences with places and stories of overlooked or often-forgotten people. Our plays aren't necessarily about history; sometimes, they might focus on science and nature or art. But they always explore and participate in grounding cultural identity, rooted in place and community.

All our projects involve partnerships with a non-profit institution. We work closely with our partners to understand the institutional needs that bring them to this collaboration. We have a multi-phase process that ensures the plays we create mesh with the stories, ideas, and resources of our partners. We work closely together at every step, from initial research to closing night, bringing a talented and experienced team of theater professionals to create plays in unusual places.

When audiences experience our work, they find new meaning in the places, topics, and people at the heart of our plays. Our work changes the way they see the sites, the stories, and perhaps even their own place in our nation. Our teams cultivate safe and brave spaces that empower artists to have fun through all stages of our process.

Plays in Place is the winner of the 2025 Excellence in Consulting Award from the National Council on Public History.

MassBike is a statewide, not-for-profit organization that advocates for policies that encourage and support community wellness, equity, and inclusion, enable sustainable growth, drive economic vitality, and reduce greenhouse gas emissions. They have extensive experience in organizing group cycling events and have organized rides and events around Kittie Knox and a diverse group of historical cycling figures and events. They believe Massachusetts will be a better place to live, work, and play if more people were riding more bikes, more often. Cycling is for everyone.